W9-BON-859

The Holiday Cookbook

LOUISE STALLARD

Other Cookbooks from Random House Value Publishing, Inc.:

As American As Apple Pie

Christmas Cookies and Candy

A Taste for Love: Romantic Meals for Two

Christmas Memories with Recipes

The Holiday Cookbook

LOUISE STALLARD

Produced by The Philip Lief Group, Inc.

GRAMERCY BOOKS
New York

This 1997 edition is published by Random House Value Publishing, Inc., by arrangement with The Philip Lief Group, Inc.

Gramercy Books and colophon are trademarks of Random House Value Publishing, Inc.

Printed in the United States of America

A CIP catalog record for this book is available from the Library of Congress

Random House Value Publishing, Inc,
New York • London • Toronto • Sydney • Auckland
http://www.randomhouse.com/

The Holiday Cookbook
ISBN: 0-517-18792-2

Acknowledgments

Compiling a book like this one is a piece of cake if one has lots of good friends who are also wonderful cooks and who are willing to share their knowledge most generously. I wish to thank Clara Bledsoe, Nancy Darlene Bledsoe, Cindy Collier, Sharyn Fitter, Selma Fleenor, Verla Gabriel, Joan Gundy, Janet Kroll, Ted Kroll, Sheila Lynch, Deanna Mahoney, Helen Marcum, Hemple Meredith, Helen Guthrie Miller, Penny Montgomery, Joanna Morris, Marie Ramsey, Ruth Scism, Maria Selig, Davora Starr, Carol Tonsing, Mary Vazquez-Amaral, and Sue Vermillion, and, of course, Julia Banks and Eva Weiss.

Contents

The Holiday Cookbook

Louise Stallard

Introduction

THE HOLIDAY IS COMING! WHAT AN UNQUALIFIED JOY FOR children, just as snow was for all of us before we got our drivers' licenses. The adults responsible for preparing holiday meals and entertainment may have a less than wholly favorable response to the coming festivities. All that food to prepare! All those people! All that cleaning and cleaning up!

Well, it's true that successful holiday entertaining takes a certain amount of work, but you can come through victorious by using recipes that work every time and by planning ahead. That means planning everything you can and doing everything you can ahead of time, thereby saving your real energy for enjoying yourself and the occasion and for those true dilemmas that no one can foresee or avoid (one of the cousins—an adult!—has measles; one of the kids fell off his bike and knocked a tooth out). Just as you need to keep something in reserve for real emergencies, you'll also want to keep a sense of proportion—not easy when serious entertaining is pressing on you. There are real emergencies; the supermarket being out of the kind of lettuce you wanted is not one of these.

Here are several key points to keep in mind:

1. The cry from the heart of every cookbook writer: *please read recipes all the way through before you begin to shop and cook.* We try to give you all information possible up front, but it is always helpful to have an overview of the entire process before you begin. Read the recipe and save yourself a lot of grief.
2. Your holiday entertaining is not a contract to act as nutrition monitor for all your guests. Yes, you hope they all have enough to eat and that they have fun, but it is not your job to see to their every food need. Some people are dif-

ficult if not impossible to have to dinner. That can't be helped. Of course, you will take reasonable precautions— you wouldn't serve roast beef to a committed vegetarian or offer sweet forbidden desserts to a diabetic—but it is the guests' responsibility to let you know their restrictions. It is your responsibility to remember them; always write such information down.

3. Keep an entertaining logbook. In it record who came to each meal or party, what you served, what went over big, what was just okay. This is the place to write information about dietary restrictions of people who have been your guests and may be again. Also, it saves you the embarrassment of serving exactly the same (no doubt wonderful) meal to the same people on consecutive visits to your place—no great tragedy, but still embarrassing. You might want to note as well which florist's flowers looked nicest, which color combinations flattered your house most. It is also a good idea to keep a running record of any missing pieces of glassware, china, silver, linen, and so forth. Then when you see a sale or someone asks what you would like as a gift, you can speak right up. So you didn't start an entertaining log years ago. It is never too late. Do it now. You will be very glad.

4. Consider hiring help. If you have access to a splendid housekeeper or a great cook whom you can hire to help, give a lot of thought to doing so. If no one of these descriptions occurs to you, consider friends who are not entertaining at the same time you are. You could have a mutual-help society—you would help a friend out, wouldn't you? Sometimes something as simple as having access to another refrigerator that is not crowded with holiday preparations is a godsend. Also remember young members of your own family and their friends; most young people want and need to earn some extra money. Check out their availability, willingness, talents. And prices! Most young people love to drive; they could be especially helpful by doing errands for you, picking up things at various stores, meeting guests arriving by train. Check their credentials (spotless driving records) and reputations.

5. Try not to get stuck doing every event for any holiday. You

might try the preemptive strike method: announce *early* to your crowd that you will be having the Christmas Eve supper (or whatever) this year and you hope they will come. Then look pleasant and expectant. Usually someone will start the ball rolling by claiming other events. If nobody does, stick to your guns and think of the joys of small, intimate occasions and eating out.

6. If others offer to help or to bring part of the menu to your party, *let* them. Have a list handy of dishes you need. Then you can say, "I always end up making dessert at the very last minute. It would be wonderful if you could bring that terrific pie you make." Being explicit could save you from many a congealed salad.

7. If you are having a big crowd, it is usually easier and wiser to have more dishes or serve more courses than to prepare caldrons of a few.

8. Every time you entertain, make a last-minute check of the refrigerator, the freezer, the pantry shelves, and the oven to make sure you have set out everything you made. If this sounds like an unnecessary suggestion, ask around and see how many of your friends have discovered the casserole for twelve sitting innocently in the refrigerator the morning after the party.

9. In this book, recipes that can't be easily doubled are noted as such. For instance, it is much easier to make two batches of cream puffs based on 1 cup flour and 4 eggs than it is to double the recipe. It is *possible* to double it, but more work than making it twice.

So, plan ahead. Make lists. Cook as early as you can. Recipes indicate whether made-ahead food should be refrigerated, frozen, or stored at room temperature. Delegate any tasks you can. And whenever possible, entertain people you really like. Bon appetit and enjoy yourself.

1

New Year's

An Elegant New Year's Eve Dinner
Far from the Maddening Crowd

HAPPY NEW YEAR! WHAT A WONDERFUL GREETING. WHAT A good wish for those we love. May yours be the best ever. As far as entertaining goes, we can help.

You must have seen the people who flock to cities for the holidays. They go to restaurants or nightclubs looking for a party, wondering where the action is. Alas, those of us a little more experienced know that you have to bring your own party; no commercial place of entertainment can provide the spirit of a celebration and the friends it needs to make it memorable. Such a place can only provide the room, the food, the wine. The real party you must provide yourself.

If, after the experience of celebrating in public, you would like to welcome the New Year more privately and in more comfort—not to mention less expensively—consider inviting a few people who mean a lot to you to a gala dinner at home. Plan to wear your best clothes; make the dinner memorable. You can later roll back the rug and dance to your hearts' content in uncrowded splendor to the music you and your crowd like best. No D.J. No intrusive band playing loud in your ear. All slow or all fast, whatever you like. You can celebrate the New Year and make wishes for each other with the best champagne at bargain rates. You will feel better in the morning.

The work for such a festival can be surprisingly easy. Just get the shopping done and start preparing early in the day so that there will be no last-minute panic.

1. December 26:
    Order the filets of beef or make sure your market will be

5

able to provide them for New Year's Eve. Specify that they be 2½ to 3 inches thick.

Be sure your market will be able to provide *large* mushrooms, at least 2½ to 3 inches in diameter.

2. December 30:

Pick up the meat and mushrooms.

Do the supermarket shopping.

If your crowd needs bread, no matter what, make a batch of Batter Roll dough (page 137) or scout local bakeries for distinguished breads. Or serve soft breadsticks from the dairy case at the supermarket: tie them into knots and bake as directed on the package. Very festive.

3. New Year's Eve:

Sauté the mushrooms; set them aside.

Take the peas out of the freezer.

Make a white sauce for the soufflé. Set the egg whites aside to come to room temperature.

Boil the eggs to serve with caviar.

Take the raspberries out of freezer if you're using frozen berries.

Make the melba toast if you are making it from scratch.

Wash the watercress, wrap it in a towel, and store it in refrigerator.

Make the French dressing for the salad (page 168) and store it in refrigerator.

4. Take a leisurely bath. Get dressed in what you plan to wear for dinner. Then take off your outer garments and cover your underwear with a big apron. (Be sure the window shades are closed.) Finish all of the preparations and dress in outer layer again.

5. Set out the caviar, open a bottle of champagne, and relax.

An Elegant New Year's Eve Dinner (for 6)

Caviar with Condiments and Melba Toast
Filets of Beef with Wild Rice
Mushrooms Filled with Pea Puree
Watercress Salad
Hot Lemon Soufflé with Cold Raspberry Sauce

Caviar

Buy as much as you can afford of the very best caviar. Beluga is usually thought most highly of, but other fish roe and American caviar are now available. A good dealer should let you taste. You don't need much—the point is to have a taste of the good stuff. Bring it home at the last minute, keep it very cold, and serve it with pride and the condiments it deserves.

Traditionally caviar is served with white toast, sieved hard-boiled egg yolks and egg whites, minced onion, and plenty of lemon wedges. The lemons are self-explanatory. Ditto the eggs and onions. You can buy melba toast (look for the type that looks like slices of tiny loaves of bread). Or you can make it:

Melba Toast

Buy a loaf of extra-thin-sliced white bread, the firm kind rather than the soft stuff we loved as children. Cut the crusts off the bread (kitchen shears are the easiest way) and cut the bread into the shapes you want: triangles, strips, small squares, whatever. Lay the bread out on an ungreased cookie sheet. Place another identical cookie sheet on top of the bread, and weigh it down with an iron skillet or another heavy pot. Put the whole arrangement in a 275°F. oven. Check in about 45 minutes or when the bread begins to smell like toast. You could simply toast the bread, but the very thin slices tend to curl a lot if they aren't held flat while they dry out. Rescue the toast from the oven when it is the shade of brown you want. Let it cool completely; then store it in an airtight container (such as a canister or a plastic bag tightly sealed) until it's needed.

Filets of Beef

For each person to be served, you will need one thick filet of beef. When you are preparing to cook the meal, take the beef out of the refrigerator so that it can lose its chill before broiling. Wipe the meat with a dry-damp paper towel. Make sure the string securing the rolled filet and its fat coating is firmly in place. When the rice is done, just before serving the meal, broil the filets. Allow 5 minutes per side for very rare beef, up to 8 or 10 minutes for well done.

Wild Rice

See page 141 for the recipe for wild rice.

Mushrooms Stuffed with Pea Puree

Any time early in the day, you can sauté the mushroom caps (save the stems for soup) and set them aside until you're ready to complete the meal.

2 large mushrooms (2½ to 3 inches in diameter) for each serving
2 tablespoons butter
1 package (10 oz.) frozen tiny peas in butter sauce

Wipe mushrooms with a damp paper towel.

Sauté mushroom caps in a heavy skillet in butter over very low heat until lightly browned on both sides. (They will give up some liquid but will reabsorb most of it while standing.) Set aside and cover until ready to complete meal.

Drop the package of frozen peas into boiling water and cook until just thawed. Open a corner of the boil-in bag and pour most of the butter sauce into a small bowl; reserve. Mash the peas to a puree by kneading the package with your hands. Cut another small opening in the bag. Pipe the pea puree into the mushroom caps as decoratively as possible. Drizzle with reserved butter sauce.

Hot Lemon Soufflé with Cold Raspberry Sauce

Hot dessert soufflés are delicious, look very impressive, and are embarrassingly easy to make. You can make this handsome dish well ahead of time up to beating the egg whites and baking it.

4 tablespoons butter
4 tablespoons flour
  Dash salt
1 cup milk
½ cup sugar
  Juice of 1 lemon
  Finely grated peel of 1 lemon
4 eggs, separated

Melt butter in the top of a double boiler over simmering water. Stir in flour and salt. Cook until smooth and thick. Add milk all at once and continue cooking, stirring often, until a thick sauce forms. Stir in sugar, lemon juice, and lemon peel. Remove from heat. When you can comfortably hold your hand on the bottom of the pan, beat in the egg yolks. Set aside at room temperature, covered, until ready to finish.

Just before you sit down to dinner, beat the egg whites, which will have come to room temperature by now, until soft peaks form. Fold into the lemon mixture. Start the oven at 400°F. Butter an ovenproof baking dish about 6 inches in diameter and 6 inches deep and sprinkle it with sugar. (The dish should have fairly straight sides, but you don't need a special soufflé dish.) Pour in the batter; trace a circle on top of the batter with the spatula in the dish about an inch inside the rim so that a topknot will rise as the soufflé cooks.

Bake the soufflé for 25 to 30 minutes until it is nicely risen and slightly browned on top. It will jiggle only slightly in the middle when done. If it is done before you are ready to eat it, turn off oven, leave oven door open a crack, and leave soufflé where it is. It should maintain its puff for 20 to 30 minutes. Display it for your guests; then spoon into small dessert dishes and serve with Cold Raspberry Sauce.

Cold Raspberry Sauce

Thaw a 10 oz. package of frozen raspberries. Press them through a sieve to remove seeds if you wish, and spoon over soufflé. If fresh raspberries are available, use a basket (usually about a pint) instead, just as they are. Rinse and drain them and decorate the servings of soufflé with them. You might offer simple, elegant cookies with the soufflé, but it really isn't necessary.

As a friend remarked, this is a special meal of simple, expensive foods. You could have more people to dinner, but the point of this small celebration is to enjoy those who are really close to you on an important occasion. You won't regret it.

Big Stand-Around New Year's Eve Party or Serene New Year's Day Reception

Sometimes small and intimate isn't in the picture. To have a great big party, you just need to work ahead and maintain a relentlessly relaxed posture.

For New Year's Eve, there is really no way around a full open bar. You can discourage excess drinking by providing options: plenty of soft drinks, eggnog (both alcoholic and non), hot mulled cider and wine, and sparkling water. Make sure there is a good supply of coffee toward the end of the evening. Or you could declare a festival and serve champagne only. The recipe for Champagne Punch will go a long way toward avoiding bankruptcy if you take this option.

If you serve alcoholic drinks to your guests, consider providing a drive-your-car-home option. If you do not have a supply of older teenagers to operate such a service (it takes two for each team: one to drive the guests home in their own cars, another to follow in a second car to bring the driver back), seek help from neighbors, local colleges, or the state employment agency. You can feed the young people (no drinking, since they are the designated safe drivers); they can dance and make themselves agreeable. You will be doing a favor for everyone: your guests, the kids you employ for the evening, and strangers who might be hurt if your guests drove home on their own. You may also cut down on involuntary overnight guests. ("Herbert, where did we put those air mattresses from last summer?")

Food can be as elaborate or as simple as you want. It is usually easier to make regular-size batches of several things than to try to prepare megabatches of a few. You know your crowd. Here are six hot and six cold party dishes that everyone will like. You may not need them all. Concentrate on the ones you think will be the biggest successes and that you can do ahead. Then dress to kill and prepare to enjoy your own party.

New Year's Eve Party or New Year's Day Reception
(for Any Number)

Sausages with Cranberry-Mustard Dip
Artichokes Parmesan   Rumaki
Cheese-Sausage Balls (page 114)   Jalapeño Pie
Deviled Miniature Kabobs
Consommé-Stuffed Mushroom Caps   Shrimp on Endive
Cherry Tomatoes Stuffed with Crabmeat Salad
Hummus with Pita Bread and Black Olives
Roast Beef or Ham Coronets
Pasta Shells Stuffed with Clams   Old Dominion Eggnog
Very Acceptable Champagne Punch
Mulled Wine or Cider

Sausages with Cranberry-Mustard Dip

    1 package (12 to 16 oz.) hot Italian sausage links
    1 package (12 to 16 oz.) sweet Italian sausage links
    1 can (10 to 12 oz.) whole-berry cranberry sauce
3 or 4 tablespoons mustard (the kind the kids put on hot dogs)

Cut the sausage links into ¾-inch slices, keeping hot and sweet sausages separate. Cover the sausages with water in separate saucepans and bring to a boil. Reduce heat so that water barely simmers. Cook 15 to 20 minutes. A *lot* of fat will come out of the sausages, making them crisper and more appealing. Drain thoroughly.

Mix cranberry sauce and mustard well. Taste. Use more mustard if you wish. Cover tightly and store in the refrigerator in a pretty dish until needed.

When you are almost ready to serve, put sausage slices on a rack over a shallow pan with sides and run under the broiler just until crisp and lightly browned. Turn and brown the other side. Arrange hot sausage on one end of a platter, sweet sausage on the other, and the sauce in the middle. Spear the sausage slices with cocktail toothpicks and make sure there are small plates or plenty of napkins available.

Hint: When people ask you about the sauce, look enigmatic and say it is an old family recipe, sacred to your Aunt Margaret or whomever. Even the most experienced cooks won't know what is in it—until after they read this book, of course.

Artichokes Parmesan

1 can (10 to 12 oz.) artichoke hearts packed in water
1 cup freshly grated Parmesan cheese
¾ cup mayonnaise

Heat oven to 325°F.

Very thoroughly drain artichoke hearts. Mince with a sharp knife or very briefly in a food processor (you want recognizable pieces).

Mix all ingredients together to blend well. Turn into a 1-cup casserole or an individual soufflé dish and bake 30 minutes.

Serve hot or at room temperature with your fanciest crackers. Use those tiny knives you got years ago and never knew what to do with. Failing that, muster the butter knives to spread the artichokes.

Hints: Each 1-cup casserole will serve about 15 people when there are lots of other good things to eat. Make several and put them in the oven as the evening progresses, or make them all at once and serve them at different spots in the party room.

The casseroles can be assembled and covered several hours before baking.

Rumaki

½ pound chicken livers
1 pound bacon
1 can (4 to 6 oz.) whole water chestnuts

Drain the chicken livers in a sieve. Cut each one into two or three pieces, removing the membranes if you can. Blot pieces with paper towels.

Cut bacon slices in thirds.

Cut water chestnuts in half.

On a work surface, lay out a strip of bacon. Put a piece of liver in the middle, top it with a chestnut half, then fold first one end of the bacon, then the other, over the liver and chestnut. Secure all with a wooden toothpick.

At serving time place rumaki on a rack above a baking pan with sides and broil about 3 inches from heat source until one side is crisp and brown. Turn (by hand is the easiest way) and brown the the other side. Drain on paper towels.

Hints: Don't worry if the little bundles look sloppy when you make them, especially the first few. The bacon will contract as it broils so that they will look quite polite when finished.

These kabobs can be made well ahead of serving time. Put them directly on the rack above the broiling pan, cover the whole arrangement tightly with foil or plastic wrap, and store in the refrigerator or another very cool place until ready to finish.

You are bound to have a little bit of something left over. These are the proportions that work best, but if you have leftover bacon and chestnuts, for instance, you can enjoy them by themselves the next day. If you have bacon and livers, use them in scrambled eggs the following morning.

Cheese-Sausage Balls

You may have some of these left in the freezer from the cooking you did for Thanksgiving and Christmas. If not, whip up a fresh batch (page 114).

Jalapeño Pie

1 can (10–12 oz.) chopped jalapeño peppers packed in
water
1 pound shredded cheddar or Monterey Jack cheese
6 eggs

Heat oven to 350°F. Thoroughly butter a 9 × 9-inch
casserole.
Drain peppers and press out any extra liquid. Grate cheese
in food processor or by hand. Beat eggs lightly.
Mix all ingredients and turn into baking dish. Bake 30
minutes; then let stand at least 15 minutes.
Cut into 1-inch squares and serve directly from baking dish.

Deviled Miniature Kabobs

2 cups raw medium to small shrimp, shelled, or roast
beef cut in ½-inch cubes, or cooked turkey cut in ½-
inch cubes
Deviled marinade (see below)
1 small package cherry tomatoes
1 can (about 10 oz.) pickled cocktail onions (the kind
sold for Gibsons)
Garnishes: lemon slices for shrimp, capers for beef,
parsley or dill for turkey

Put the shrimp, beef, or turkey into a small dish or plastic
bag. Cover with marinade and let stand 2 to 3 hours or
overnight.
Marinade: Combine ½ cup olive oil with 3 tablespoons
lemon juice, 2 tablespoons Dijon mustard, salt and pepper to
taste, ¼ teaspoon tarragon, and a dash of hot pepper sauce.
Mix well and pour over shrimp or meat.
Just before serving time retrieve shrimp or meat from marinade and shake free of excess liquid; do not blot. Arrange
meat, cherry tomatoes, and onions alternately on sturdy
wooden toothpicks. There will probably be only two or three
pieces of meat on each toothpick; this is a tiny treat, not a
meal. Arrange kabobs on a rack over a shallow pan with sides
and broil 3 inches from heat source until shrimp turns pink or

other meats are hot, more than 3 or 4 minutes a side. Brush with marinade if meat looks dry.

To serve, put broiling rack directly on a heatproof platter, garnish, and serve.

Hint: This could help you use up the leftovers from Thanksgiving and Christmas. You could also start with boneless chicken breasts—same prescription as shrimp.

Now for the cold goodies. The beauty of cold or room-temperature appetizers is that they can be made well ahead and will look just as lovely and welcoming hours after you prepare them.

Consommé-Stuffed Mushroom Caps

1 pound mushrooms at least 2 inches in diameter
1 can beef consommé, jelled (or, if consommé is
unavailable, 1½ cups beef or chicken broth jelled with
1 envelope unflavored gelatin)
Garnishes (optional): lumpfish caviar, lemon slices,
slices of hard-boiled egg, parsley, minced onion

Wipe mushrooms with a damp paper towel. Remove stems and save for another use. Set caps aside, covered.

Check consommé. If it is not really stiff, heat, strengthen with gelatin, and reset. If you are using broth, soften gelatin in a few tablespoons of cold broth, then heat until no granules appear on the back of a spoon. Mix with remainder of broth and chill in a shallow pan at least 2 hours or until firmly set.

When ready to assemble, cut consommé into very small bite-sized pieces with two knives or a fork. Pile into mushroom caps. Arrange stuffed mushrooms on a serving platter and garnish as you wish.

Hints: Your calorie-watching friends will praise you for serving this pretty, tasty treat. It is practically free of sin. A little sodium, yes; fat and cholesterol, no.

The jelled filling of the mushrooms holds up surprisingly well in a party room, though you might want to position it away from radiators, the sound system, and hot lights.

Shrimp on Endive

This is another treat that dieters will appreciate. It is pretty, elegant, and hasn't enough calories to make up for the dancing they'll be doing later.

½ **pound tiny cooked salad shrimp, or 1 can (6 to 8 oz.)
   tiny shrimp**
4 **heads endive
   Mayonnaise
   Caviar (optional)
   Cherry tomatoes
   Parsley
   Fresh dill**

Keep cooked tiny shrimp from the fish market very cold until you are ready to assemble this dish.

Drain canned shrimp if you are using them. Blot with paper towels to be sure they have no brine left clinging. Keep cold.

Fearlessly cut ½ inch off the bottoms of the heads of endive. Separate the leaves, wash, then dry them thoroughly.

When you're ready to assemble the platter, put ½ teaspoon (use a measuring spoon to keep quantity uniform) mayonnaise on each endive leaf at the stem end. Place 1 or 2 tiny shrimp on top of the mayonnaise. Top with caviar if you wish. Arrange on platter and garnish with cherry tomatoes, parsley, and dill.

Hints: If you love to make mayonnaise, by all means use your own. However, this is not the time to acquire a new skill. If you find your commercial mayo a little shy, try adding a tablespoon of lemon juice per cup. Stir like crazy. You could also spike up the canned product with some finely minced fresh dill—very well thought of in poultry circles.

Yes, endive is expensive, but it produces a great effect. Worth it this time.

Cherry Tomatoes Stuffed with Crabmeat Salad

Stuffed cherry tomatoes are good to eat, cute, and festive. This recipe incorporates a standard crabmeat salad. You can also use it to stuff tiny cream puffs, sandwiches, quiche, or whatever your heart desires. There is only one caution on the tomatoes: don't even think of hollowing them out and stuffing the shells. That takes too long. I tried it once, starting at the first blush of dawn and finishing just as the earliest guests appeared. Take the quick way out.

1 **pound cherry tomatoes**
½ **pound fresh cooked crabmeat or 1 can (8 oz.) crabmeat**
¼ **cup finely diced celery, including some leaves**
¼ **cup finely minced scallion, including some of the green part**
2 **to 3 tablespoons mayonnaise (enough to moisten)**
½ **teaspoon dry mustard**
1 **teaspoon lemon juice**
Salt and pepper
Parsley sprigs

Wash and drain tomatoes well. For prettier goodies, cut them in half from top to bottom and leave the green stem on. If you want no-garbage pickup bites, remove the green stem and cut the tomatoes in half crosswise.

Check crabmeat and remove all bones, shells, and cartilage. In a medium-size bowl combine the remaining ingredients except parsley and mix well, breaking up the crabmeat in the process. Do not overmix.

Put a ½ teaspoon crab salad on each tomato. If you have very large cherry tomatoes, use a little more. You want a succulent bite, not a mess.

Arrange stuffed tomatoes on a platter and garnish with parsley sprigs or whatever appeals to you.

Hints: To stuff cream puffs: with this crab salad, cut the puffs in half and fill them sandwich-style instead of trying to inject them.

This salad also makes very, very good sandwiches on good whole wheat bread.

To use in quiche, spread crab salad in the bottom of the unbaked piecrust and pour custard mixture over the top. Very fine and unusual.

You really *must* alert your guests to the presence of shellfish in any dish you serve. There are more and more people allergic to fish and shellfish—alas, especially crab. Make labels—placecards work well. Be sure people who are helping themselves to platters being passed know what they are eating. Allergic reactions can be serious, sometimes life-threatening (asthmatic attacks and cardiac arrest). You have other treats they can sample. Let them know which are which.

Hummus with Pita Bread and Black Olives

There is a lot of mystification about hummus. In fact, it is simplicity itself. Truly a case of less is more.

1 can (16 oz.) chick-peas (garbanzos)
3–4 garlic cloves, peeled and roughly chopped
½ cup olive oil
Juice of 1 or 2 lemons
8 pita bread rounds cut into thin wedges
Black olives
Parsley (optional)
Salt

Drain the beans, reserving the liquid. Put the beans, garlic, olive oil, and lemon juice into a blender. Add some liquid from the beans if more fluid is needed. Make a smooth puree. Taste and add salt and a little more olive oil if needed.

That's it. Nothing mysterious. Serve with a basket of pita wedges (you could warm them, but it really doesn't matter). Black olives are the traditional garnish. Very good, too. Add parsley, if you like it.

Hints: If you want to cook the chick-peas from scratch, by all means do. Follow package directions, or if there aren't any, wash, look over, and soak the chick-peas overnight in a large pot with water to cover by at least 2 inches. Then drain, cover again with water, add 1 teaspoon salt, and simmer them until tender. Proceed as above. I have tried cooking chick-peas from the beginning, and I found that they taste remarkably like the canned ones. You do your own thing.

Use scissors to cut the pita into wedges.

Roast Beef or Ham Coronets

Now is the time to take any leftover roast beef or ham out of the freezer and use it to good account. If you don't have any of these treasures, make a trip to the local deli.

24 thin 4 × 4-inch slices beef or ham
 8 ounces ricotta cheese
   Parsley or fresh dill (optional)
   Cherry tomatoes (optional)

Lay out slices of meat on a work surface. If you have very agile fingers, form a cone from each slice of meat, fill it with ricotta, and secure with a toothpick if it looks shaky. If you are less digitally gifted, wrap meat around a little cone-shaped paper cup to form a coronet, slip it off, and fill it with cheese.

That's all there is to that. Pretty, hearty, and virtually free, since you probably had the meat on hand. Arrange the coronets on a platter and garnish with parsley, dill, or cherry tomatoes, if you wish—or use whatever you have to brighten it up.

Pasta Shells Stuffed with Clams

At a very grand party several years ago, the guests appeared to be eating clam shells whole. Who on earth was their dentist? The dish turned out to very large pasta shells stuffed with clams. A very good no-waste treat.

1 pound large pasta shells
2 cans (16 oz. each) cooked minced clams, well drained
¼ cup finely chopped celery
¼ cup finely chopped onion
2 tablespoons fresh bread crumbs or wheat germ
2–3 tablespoons mayonnaise
  Salt and freshly ground pepper to taste
  Lemon wedges

Cook pasta shells according to package directions. When they are just tender, drain and return to cooking pot with a teaspoon or two of olive oil and stir well. The oil keeps the pasta from sticking together. If you cook pasta ahead of time, store in the refrigerator.

When you're ready to assemble this dish, mix the remaining ingredients and pile the mixture into the pasta shells. Arrange the stuffed shells on serving dishes and garnish with lemon wedges.

Now to the drinkables. If your punches go over well, you may not have as much alcohol consumption as you would otherwise. This is not a particularly light eggnog recipe, but it is the real thing. It is quite filling, so hardly anyone can drink it endlessly.

Old Dominion Eggnog

  6 **eggs, separated**
¾ **cup sugar**
  2 **cups heavy cream**
2½ **cups milk**
  1 **pint bourbon**
¼ **cup dark rum (optional)**
    Freshly grated nutmeg

Beat egg yolks with ½ cup of the sugar until sugar is all dissolved.

Beat egg whites to firm but soft peaks. Add the remaining ¼ cup sugar and make sure it is all dissolved.

Mix eggs together and gently add cream and milk. Add bourbon and rum a little at a time, and mix well.

Tightly cover and chill the mixture thoroughly before serving. Eggnog should be made at least 24 hours before it is to be served. It will keep for five or six days in the refrigerator, getting better all the time. Grate nutmeg over each serving.

Hints: This recipe makes about 2 quarts eggnog. Each serving should be small. Drag out your punch bowl and all those little cups. It is also a nice gesture to have an extra pitcher of cold milk alongside in case people want to thin down this rather intense mixture.

For nonalcoholic eggnog, I don't think you can do better than to buy the mixture sold in the dairy case. Again, provide milk to cut thickness.

Very Acceptable Champagne Punch

Have all ingredients and the punch bowl or pitcher very cold. You can mix the non-sparkling ingredients ahead of time, but add the champagne the last minute, just before you serve the punch.

1 bottle (8 oz.) tonic water
¼ cup fresh lemon juice, strained
1 bottle (750 ml.) dry white wine
2 bottles (750 ml. each) brut champagne
1 quart ginger ale
1 quart club soda or seltzer
  Lemon-peel curls, strawberries, or other garnishes

Mix all ingredients very, very gently so as not to dissipate the bubbles. Serve the punch in champagne glasses with garnishes.

Hints: You don't need to use terrifically good wine and champagne for this punch, but it should be respectable—something you would drink on its own. Just think how much mileage you're getting out of it.

A lovely accent for the punch bowl is a ring of ice (use your tube pan or bundt pan and boiled water) with some little blossoms or fruit frozen inside. Ladle the cooled water into the mold gently to minimize the white spots that air causes.

Bite the bullet and squeeze that lemon juice fresh. It matters here.

On a cold night, very few things are as welcome as a mug of hot mulled wine or cider. It is a snap to make.

Mulled Wine or Cider

2 quarts decent but not precious red wine or 2 quarts good apple cider
2 cinnamon sticks
3 whole cloves
1 whole allspice
3 whole black peppercorns

Pour the wine or cider into a nonmetal saucepan (enamel, or the glass or Pyrex pans made specifically for stove top use). Tie the spices up in a square of cheesecloth or put them in a ceramic tea ball.

Heat the wine or cider gently over low to medium heat just until bubbles begin to form at the edges of the pan. Add the spice package, cover, turn the heat to the lowest possible level, and let the liquid steep for at least 15 minutes. Keep the heat very low; do not let wine boil.

Serve this beverage in cups with a handle—mulled wine or cider can make a glass too hot to hold comfortably. Enjoy.

Hint: You can make mulled white wine as well, but it suffers from an odd cosmetic defect—it doesn't look good. I tried it only once.

New Year's Breakfast

Your last good deed for New Year's Eve may be to feed the very last party animals a substantial breakfast so they can face the year ahead with a better outlook.

Matzo Brei

Matzo brei is a great recipe when you have five people and four eggs. It's a very tasty, sort of unusual combination of eggs, bread, and anything else you would like to see go to a good home.

This recipe will serve about 6 people.

3 whole matzo crackers or 8 water biscuits
6 eggs
2 tablespoons butter
Salt and pepper

Roughly break up the crackers. Cover with tepid water and let stand a few minutes. When you're ready, drain the crackers and squeeze out most of the liquid.

Break the eggs into a bowl and stir to mix yolks and whites. Add drained crackers and mix just to acquaint the two; don't overmix.

Melt the butter in a large skillet over medium heat. When the butter bubbles, add the egg mixture. Move it around with a spatula until the eggs are scrambled as you like. Don't overcook. Serve with salt and pass the pepper mill.

Hints: If you need something to push the matzo brei around, bagels are probably best, but toast, English muffins, or anything along those lines will taste good, too.

"Protestant" matzo brei can be made with water biscuits, the kind sold at vast expense as a shelf for caviar, outrageously expensive cheese, and dips you don't really want to know about. But they are sometimes available where matzos are not. A box of them in the pantry is good insurance for all sorts of entertaining emergencies. They look so darned polite, and they sure do make good matzo brei.

If you have any of the breads you made for Christmas, remember them. Now is a golden time to push the last of the cranberry bread or the apricot loaf, whatever you still have in the fridge. If there isn't anything (usually the case), you may want to consider making a coffee cake.

Exceptionally Fast Coffeecake

2 cups flour
3 teaspoons baking powder
½ cup sugar
½ cup melted butter or margarine
1 cup milk
2 eggs
½ cup brown sugar
1 tablespoon cinnamon

Grease a 9 × 9-inch baking pan. Heat oven to 375°F.
Mix all ingredients except brown sugar and cinnamon.
Pour batter into prepared pan. Toss brown sugar and cinnamon together to mix and sprinkle on top of batter. Bake 20 minutes, or until a cake tester comes out clean. Cut into squares and serve at once; it will stick to the pan if the brown-sugar stuff cools there.

New Year's Day Bowl-Game Party

If you had a New Year's Eve party, you should be excused from any further exertions for a week, but sometimes the ideal is not the actual. If your friends are football fans and it is your turn to have the bowl-game party, I'm afraid you're for it. Plan better next year.

If your friends don't know the difference between the coin toss and the goalpost and don't care, consider a nice quiet late afternoon or very early evening reception. Many people feel let down on New Year's Day. After all the festivities of the preceding weeks, everything can seem bleak. A sweet, comforting get-together with friends could make life nicer.

Serve whatever seems suitable from the New Year's Eve menu. Specialize in coffee and tea to drink. If it is a whole new group, think of the champagne punch. This is not the moment for an open bar; by now everyone's digestive system needs a break.

If the bowl-game party is your responsibility, tuck up your courage. It can be fun, too. You need food that can be made ahead, dishes that wait gracefully for erratic time-outs. You can use all of the ones mentioned below if some year the Super Bowl party falls on you.

Also, don't forget the obvious: cheese and crackers, popcorn, chips and dips. No matter what culinary heights you rise to, someone is sure to remember your party as the one with the splendid California dip and the exceptionally crisp chips. The obvious drink is beer; tuck a good supply of nonalcoholic beer into the cooler, too. And soft drinks. It is now time to ease up on the holiday spirits.

You will need to do some work between Christmas and New Year's to bring this occasion off. Not the jolliest prospect, but these recipes are easy, and most benefit from being made ahead, and others don't take enough time to discuss.

1. As soon as you can face the kitchen after Christmas, make sauce for Turkey Lasagna and prepare the lasagna. Cover tightly and freeze. If you wish to prepare the lasagna on party day, you can simply store the sauce in an airtight container in the refrigerator until needed.
2. If you have vegetarian guests, make a batch of Vegetarian Chili (page 108).
3. Make Reliable Beef Stew while you are in the kitchen working on the Turkey Lasagna. This stew just gets better for up to a week when stored in the refrigerator.
4. Do the basic shopping for the rest of the food. Buy the black-eyed peas when you see them, as early as possible. It is traditional to eat them for good luck on New Year's sometimes markets get sold out, especially in the South and the West.

Bowl-Game Party (for Any Number)

Turkey Lasagna   Vegetarian Chili (page 108)
Reliable Beef Stew   Seafood Fondue
Chicken Wings with Three Dips   Nachos
Black-Eyed Peas   Corn Bread

Make as many of these dishes as you feel your crowd will enjoy and need. Just keep in mind that your guests may start arriving for the easternmost parade and stay until the bitter end of the Rose Bowl. An enthusiastic bunch of fans can eat an enormous amount. Each recipe provides about ten servings. Note that that is *servings,* not the number of people served.

Turkey Lasagna

This recipe has everything: it is delicious, it is easy, it has almost no fat or cholesterol. Everybody likes it. It is better made ahead. The sauce also makes very, very good eggplant Parmesan, spaghetti, and all the usual Italian red sauce dishes. Keep some in the freezer; think of it as your food tax-free bonds.

Lasagna Sauce

 3 pounds ground turkey
 3 really large onions
 6 cloves garlic
 1 can (28 oz.) whole plum tomatoes
 2 cans (15 oz. each) tomato sauce (*not* tomato paste!)
 2 whole bay leaves
 ½ teaspoon ground cinnamon
 ½ cup chopped fresh parsley
 1 teaspoon dried basil
 ½ teaspoon dried rosemary
 ½ teaspoon oregano

In a large heavy pot with a tight-fitting lid, cook the turkey over medium heat until it loses its pink color. It won't exactly brown; it will just give up some juice. Stir with a wooden spoon to break up chunks of meat.

Peel and roughly chop onions and garlic. Add to turkey and cook until onions are wilted.

Add tomatoes and tomato sauce. Rinse the cans out with a little water to get all the juice and add the water to the pot. Add spices and herbs. Simmer, uncovered, about 2 hours, stirring occasionally.

Taste sauce and add salt and pepper if desired. If the sauce seems a little sharp, add a teaspoon of sugar; if it is very sweet (tomatoes vary), add a little red wine vinegar. Continue simmering, covered, for another hour.

When sauce is done, cool and refrigerate or freeze, or assemble the lasagna and store or freeze it.

Lasagna Casserole

  1 **pound lasagna noodles (12 to 16 whole long noodles)**
  1 **teaspoon salt**
    Olive oil
 16 **ounces ricotta cheese**
 16 **ounces mushrooms, cleaned and roughly chopped**
 16 **ounces mozzarella cheese, shredded or thinly sliced**
  8 **ounces grated Romano or Parmesan cheese**

Cook lasagna until tender in salted water. Drain and rinse in cool water, then drain again. Set aside until cool enough to handle.

Lightly brush the bottom and sides of two 9 × 13 × 2-inch baking dishes with olive oil. This is the only oil in the whole dish, but it makes a lot of difference to the taste. Put a dollop of sauce in the bottom of each dish and spread it around. Lay out one layer of noodles, overlapping edges slightly.

Spoon half the ricotta on top of noodles in each dish; it will spread itself around in the finished lasagnas. Spoon half the mushrooms on top of ricotta in each dish. Cover all with a layer of sauce. Top with a quarter of the mozzarella.

Add another layer of noodles, the rest of the sauce, mozzarella, and Romano or Parmesan, dividing the ingredients between the two dishes.

Cook the lasagnas for 30 minutes in a 350°F. oven. If the finished lasagna has been refrigerated, bake it for an hour; if it was frozen, it will need at least an hour, maybe 1½ hours, in the oven.

Hint: The assembly sounds more complicated than it is. You want layers of (small amounts of) sauce, noodles, ricotta, mushrooms, sauce, mozzarella, noodles, sauce, mozzarella, grated hard cheese. If you get some of the layers out of order, who would know? Who would tell? It might even taste better. Not to worry.

Reliable Beef Stew

2 pounds stewing beef in 1-inch chunks
  Flour
  Salt and pepper
1 teaspoon dried oregano
2 tablespoons butter or margarine
1 large onion, peeled and roughly chopped
3 cups beef broth or 3 cups water with 3 low-sodium
  bouillon cubes
3 large baking potatoes, scrubbed but not peeled
4 large carrots, scrubbed but not peeled
  Chopped fresh parsley
½ cup chopped celery (optional)

In a paper or plastic bag, dredge the cubes of stew beef in a mixture of flour, salt, pepper, and oregano. Melt butter in a heavy casserole with a tight-fitting lid. Brown meat on all sides.

Dredge onion in flour mixture. Pile meat to one side of casserole and add onion. Add a little more butter if necessary. The onions do not need to brown, but they should be wilted and almost soft.

Add broth to casserole. Bring to a boil, then reduce heat so stew barely simmers. Cook, covered, for 30 minutes.

Cut potatoes and carrot into 1-inch chunks. Add to stew. Return mixture to a vigorous boil; reduce heat and simmer for 1 hour. Check potatoes. They should be very tender. Give the stew a good stir with a wooden spoon to break up some of the potatoes to thicken the mixture.

The stew is now ready to eat, but it will be much, much better if it is allowed to cool. Store in the refrigerator. If any fat rises to the top, take it off (it will be easy since it will be solid).

To serve, garnish with parsley and add celery for crunch, if you wish.

Hint: For extra zest, you can add mushrooms and use red wine for part of the liquid. All sorts of variations are possible, but the basic stew is quite delectable enough. Try it.

Seafood Fondue

This recipe is embarrassingly simple, but it serves a purpose: those guests who would like something that is not based on red meat but who are not strict vegetarians will bless you for it. It also tastes wonderful and is infinitely flexible.

This is the time to haul out your chafing dish. Polish up the top container, not the one that will later hold hot water, and hold for action. A votive candle in a custard cup will keep everything hot later on if you have as little success as I do with those little alcohol lamps.

½ **pound processed cheese**
½ **cup minced onion**
½ **cup minced celery**
 2 **tablespoons finely chopped fresh parsley**
 2 **tablespoons butter**
½ **cup milk**
  Salt and pepper
 1 **teaspoon dry mustard**
  Fresh lemon juice (optional)
2½ **cups tuna, crabmeat, and/or shrimp**

Shred the cheese or cut it into very small pieces.

In the top container of a chafing dish, cook the onion and celery and parsley in the butter until they are wilted. Add the shredded cheese and the milk. The cheese will melt very slowly, but that is fine. When the mixture is fairly smooth, add salt and pepper to taste and stir in the dry mustard. You might want to add a squeeze of fresh lemon juice as well. Taste and see. Put boiling water in the bottom container of the chafing dish and put top pan over it over heat source.

Drain canned seafood thoroughly and cut into small pieces. Add it to the cheese mixture and heat slowly, very gently. Serve the fondue over rice or with chunks of French bread to dip on long forks.

Hints: The etiquette of fondue eating dictates that if someone drops a chunk of bread into the fondue he or she has to kiss everybody at the table. Use your own judgment.

You could use real cheddar or a more elegant cheese, but processed cheese is the one that always melts perfectly.

It takes some time to melt and heat everything for this recipe, but it requires no attention. You could truly paint the barn while preparing this recipe and nothing would go wrong with the fondue. Just add the seafood last.

Any available seafood will taste good in this dish. Use canned or leftover seafood if you wish.

Chicken Wings with Three Dips

Not only is this recipe simple; it also gives you a very nice dividend of chicken broth to use in other dishes.

2 pounds chicken wings
1 small onion stuck with a whole clove
1 large carrot, scrubbed and cut into 1-inch chunks
2 celery stalks, roughly chopped
2 garlic cloves, halved
2 bay leaves

Wash and drain the chicken wings. Tuck the tip of each wing behind the first joint to make a neat triangle.

Put chicken into a large soup pot and add the rest of the ingredients. Cover with water by at least 1½ inches. Bring to a boil; lower heat and simmer for about 30 minutes. (This is also a good opportunity to use up any chicken giblets you may have in the freezer.)

Rescue the chicken wings when they are barely tender. If any frozen extra giblets are fully cooked, strain the broth and let it cool. Skim off all the fat that will rise to the top. Freeze the broth and extra giblets for later use. Store chicken wings in the refrigerator until you are ready to finish them.

When ready to prepare for the party, broil chicken wings on a rack over a baking pan until they are lightly browned and crisp on both sides: about 5 minutes per side. Drain on paper towels. Now you can make the dipping sauces.

Buffalo Chicken-Wing Sauce

A few years ago a fad for Buffalo Chicken Wings swept the country. There is a good reason this food was so successful: it tastes good. There is no mystery involved, however. Here's how to make the sauce.

1 pint sour cream
2 tablespoons mayonnaise
3 ounces blue cheese, crumbled
  Neatly trimmed celery sticks

Mix sour cream, mayonnaise, and blue cheese. Store in a tightly covered pretty dish in the refrigerator. Prepare the celery sticks and store them in a plastic bag in the refrigerator. Serve hot, crisp chicken wings with sauce and celery for dipping and munching.

Mustard-Honey Sauce

This is our old chum from the Chinese restaurant.

½ cup honey
1 tablespoon dry mustard
  Lemon juice or lime juice (optional)

Mix honey with mustard and taste. If sauce is too hot for you, add more honey. If it is not spicy enough, add more mustard. If the sauce is too thick, dilute with a little lemon juice or lime juice.

Hint: You might also like a less intense version of this sauce, made by combining apricot jam with mustard to taste. Very subtle. These sauces taste better at room temperature.

Vaguely Oriental Sauce That Tastes Good

1 tablespoon butter
1 tablespoon vegetable oil
¼ cup soy sauce

Melt the butter. Mix with oil and soy sauce and beat hard. (A whisk is probably the best implement for mixing this sauce.)

Hints: Make more sauce if you need it. It should stay liquid after mixed, but it isn't great after standing for a long period.

This sauce is also very good on vegetables, especially broccoli.

Nachos

It is a little more trouble to make the real things, but not much.

1 bag (10 or 16 oz.) unbroken taco chips
1 can refried beans
1 tablespoon ground cumin
Salt and pepper
1 can sliced jalapeños packed in water
8 ounces Monterey Jack cheese
Hot salsa

Lay out the taco chips (unsalted ones are very good here) on a serving platter. If you intend to heat them in a microwave, use a microwave-safe platter; if you are going to finish the nachos in a conventional oven, use a metal or heatproof ceramic dish. Chips should be in one layer.

Empty canned refried beans into a mixing bowl and stir in cumin. Taste and add salt and pepper if you wish. The cumin goes a long way toward revitalizing canned beans.

Drain jalapeño slices thoroughly. Cut cheese into airmail-stamp-sized thin slices. Put the salsa into a serving dish.

Put about 2 teaspoons of beans on the cupped side of each taco chip. Add a slice of jalapeño. Top with a piece of cheese. Do not overload chips; they will be hard to eat if you do. Put chips on their serving platter in the microwave for 1 minute or in a conventional oven for 5 to 10 minutes at 400°F. Everything in this dish is cooked; you only need to melt the cheese and heat everything through. Serve with salsa.

Hint: Make several platters of nachos. Heat one platter at a time, as needed. If you put them all out at once, the nachos will get cold and chewy—not the effect you wish to create.

Black-Eyed Peas

It is supposed to be good luck to eat black-eyed peas on New Year's Day. I certainly hope so, since I have dutifully had a bite for years and I don't really like them. Many people do like them, however, and they make a nice substantial dish for a party.

1 pound dried black-eyed peas
¼ pound salt pork or unsmoked bacon
2 teaspoons salt, or to taste

Soak the peas overnight with water to cover by about 2 inches (the alternative method is to cook them longer on the stove). Drain off excess water.

Score (cut almost through as though slicing) the salt pork. In a large heavy pot with a lid, brown the meat on all sides over medium heat. A good bit of fat will cook out of the meat, and you will need it to flavor the peas.

Add the drained peas. Cover by at least 2 inches with water and add about half the salt you will eventually use, say 2 teaspoons. The cooking water should be *slightly* salty. Bring peas to a boil, then reduce heat so that the pot simmers gently. Partially cover and cook for 1 to 2 hours. Check the water level from time to time and add liquid if necessary. When peas are very tender, taste them and add more salt, if necessary. Let the pot boil hard for a few minutes, uncovered, to thicken the mixture somewhat.

Hint: These are basic black-eyed peas. They are usually served in a soup bowl accompanied by raw onion slices. Pass the pepper grinder. You can also add a slice of pork roast or perhaps some diced leftover ham to each bowl. Or you could with very little more effort make one of the dozens of versions of Hopping John (or Hoppin' Jon—it has as many different names as there are recipes). You can't go wrong by adding 3 sliced carrots, 1 chopped onion, 2 stalks chopped celery, and a bay leaf to the pot 45 minutes before the beans are done. You can use the same procedure to cook Great Northern or navy beans, in which case you will have made White Bean Soup. Very good, too.

Corn Bread

The traditional bread to serve with dried beans or peas is nonsweet corn bread. This bread is also the base of many stuffings. It is fast and easy to make.

3 tablespoons vegetable shortening
1½ cups white cornmeal
¼ cup flour
¾ teaspoons salt
1½ teaspoons baking powder
⅔ cup milk (approx.)

Heat the oven to 450°F. Put the vegetable shortening into an 8-inch black cast-iron skillet and set the skillet in the oven, to get very hot and to melt the shortening.

Sift the dry ingredients together. Pour the melted shortening from the skillet into them, and add the milk, and stir just to mix well. The batter should be fairly thick but not stiff; it should flow when poured without being runny. If the batter seems dry, add a little more milk or rinse out the milk cup with water and add that.

Pour batter into the hot skillet and bake 20 to 25 minutes. The top should be nicely browned. Turn out of skillet onto a serving plate and serve hot with butter.

Hint: If you don't have a black cast-iron skillet, use the heaviest cake pan you own.

If you feel you must offer some dessert, empty out the supply from Christmas—fruitcake, cookies, whatever you have—or shamelessly buy something. You've done quite enough.

2

♡ ♡ ♡ ♡ ♡ ♡ ♡ ♡ ♡ ♡

Valentine's Day

A Romantic Dinner for Two

AT THIS MOST ROMANTIC HOLIDAY, OUR HEARTS TURN TO thoughts of, well, romance. While it may not be strictly true that the way to the heart is through the stomach, good food can certainly set an atmosphere of caring and ease. Comfort food is especially nice for this purpose. This Valentine's Day menu has clinched several happy unions.

A Romantic Dinner (for 2)

Consommé Madrilène
Pot Roast with Gravy Stroganoff
Fresh Pasta Dumplings
Asparagus with Tiny Onions
Coeur à la Crème with Strawberries

Consommé Madrilène

You could make tomato-flavored consommé from scratch, but the canned variety is very good. Heat the consommé gently according to the instructions on the can. Garnish each bowl with a little chopped tomato and a sprig of whatever fresh green herb you can find. If your market does not have Madrilène, buy beef consommé and follow this recipe:

1 can (10 oz.) beef consommé
1 large or 2 small plum tomatoes, peeled, seeded, and
　chopped
1 teaspoon dried basil
1 teaspoon tarragon
3 tablespoons tomato juice
　Chopped fresh tomato
　Sprigs of fresh green herbs

In a heavy saucepan combine the first four ingredients. Heat gently for 15 minutes. Strain.

Return consommé to saucepan, add tomato juice, and heat again.

Serve in bouillon cups garnished with chopped tomato and sprigs of herbs.

Pot Roast with Gravy Stroganoff

This dish has everything for seduction: it is homey, non-threatening, delicious, and so easy it is embarrassing.

1 eye of round or other good pot roast (3 or 4 lb.)
1 can cream of mushroom soup
1 envelope dry onion soup mix
1 cup (8 oz.) sour cream

In an ovenproof and heatproof casserole with a lid, gently brown the meat on all sides.

Add the undiluted mushroom soup. Sprinkle with dry onion soup mix. Cover and cook over very low heat or in a 300°F. oven for 2 to 3 hours, until the meat is tender when pierced with a skewer. A meat thermometer should register about 140°F. minimum. (Pot roast should never be really rare.)

When meat is done and you are ready to serve the meal, transfer the roast to a serving platter and keep it warm in a 250°F. oven. Add sour cream to the gravy in the casserole. Stir and heat until smooth. To serve, slice meat and serve with the gravy and Fresh Pasta Dumplings.

Fresh Pasta Dumplings

The beauty of dumplings is that you get the fresh flavor but don't have to go through the rolling-out process that is required for homemade pasta.

1½ cups flour, sifted
2 eggs
Salt
Butter or margarine

Combine flour and unbeaten eggs in the container of a food processor fitted with the steel blade. Process until dough forms a ball, then pulse another time or two. You have now accomplished the kneading.

If you do not have a food processor (a blender won't work for this recipe), combine flour and eggs in a large bowl and beat very hard with a wooden spoon or mix with your hands just until you can form the dough into a ball. Knead the dough on a board until it is smooth.

Bring a large pot of lightly salted (1 teaspoon salt to each quart) water to a boil. Reduce heat so that water just simmers. Pinch off bits of dough about ¾ inch in diameter and drop them into the water. Add dumplings a few at a time so that water never stops simmering. Do not crowd the dumplings. They will puff up as they cook—not much, but some. The dumplings will first sink, then rise as they cook. Turn them with a slotted spoon when they rise. Let them cook another 3 or 4 minutes. Then drain and put into a serving dish with a little butter or margarine to keep them from sticking together.

Hint: You will no doubt have some meat and possibly some pasta left over. Freeze it for later use. You will not regret it.

Asparagus with Tiny Onions

The first pencil-slim asparagus of the season should be available about now. If it isn't, you can use frozen asparagus. Fresh is better.

1 pound asparagus
1 package (10 oz.) tiny frozen creamed onions
Grated Parmesan cheese (optional)

Wash and drain the asparagus and break off the tough lower ends of the stems. (Hold each stalk in your hands; bend gently. It will break in the right place.) Steam the spears over a small amount of water just until the asparagus is tender-crisp.

If you are using frozen asparagus, take it out of the freezer in time to thaw completely and come to room temperature. It won't need any further cooking for this dish.

Cook creamed onions according to package directions.

Arrange asparagus in one layer on an ovenproof serving platter and pour creamed onions over it. A little grated Parmesan would be nice but isn't really necessary for the taste. Run the platter under the broiler for a very few minutes to lightly brown the cream sauce.

Coeur à la Crème with Strawberries

This delicious dessert is basically enhanced cream cheese. It is beautiful and madly romantic, but not everybody has come across it before.

Individual and recipe-size coeur molds are available. Usually these are heart-shaped ceramic dishes with a lot of little drainage holes in the bottom so that the whey from the cheeses can drain away. You can also buy little baskets meant to serve the same purpose. The ceramic molds are a pain to wash, though they are so attractive that they're suitable for hanging on the kitchen wall. The baskets must be discarded after a use or two; there is no way to get all the milk products out of the straw, and they get very odd indeed. Heart-shaped cake pans work very well. Just line the pan with several layers of cheesecloth and pour off the liquid that collects several times as the coeur matures (overnight, minimum). If you don't have a heart-shaped pan or dish, use a round mold or a small loaf pan. It's the taste that counts.

8 ounces cream cheese
8 ounces farmer's cheese, cottage cheese, or ricotta
1 cup heavy cream
   Salt (optional)
1 pint strawberries
3 tablespoons sugar (approx.)
   Cointreau (optional)
   Cookies (optional)

Let the cream cheese come to room temperature to soften. Combine cheeses and cream in a mixing bowl with a wooden spoon. Stir and beat until the mixture is very smooth. Taste. You may or may not want to add a dash of salt.

Line a 3- to 4-cup mold with several layers of cheesecloth. Pile the cheese mixture into the mold and smooth down with the wooden spoon. Cover mold with foil and refrigerate overnight at least. Carefully pour off whey from coeur several times. If you are using baskets or the molds that drain through holes, be sure to put them into a pan with sides to catch the liquid. Empty the pan several times.

If fresh strawberries are available, save 3 or 4 of the prettiest ones for garnish and slice the rest. Stir the sliced berries with sugar to taste. Add a tablespoon or so of Cointreau or other fruit-flavored liqueur if you wish. Serve the berries in a small sauceboat.

Carefully unmold the coeur à la crème. Decorate with the most beautiful berries and pass the sliced berries. Small elegant cookies make a nice accompaniment, but they are really not necessary.

Hint: You will have some coeur left over. Store it, tightly covered. It is splendid spread for cocktail crackers or for your morning toast or bagel. Come to think of it, why not a romantic Valentine's Day brunch? Be creative.

As a matter of policy, champagne throughout the meal sounds right. If you have a fine old Burgundy hanging around that would complement the Stroganoff, I would be the last to dissuade you from serving it.

3

♣ ♣ ♣ ♣ ♣ ♣ ♣ ♣ ♣ ♣

Saint Patrick's Day

A Family Dinner

IF EVER THERE WAS A FAMILY HOLIDAY, SAINT PATRICK'S DAY is it. In fact, it is the family holiday of a whole people, the Irish, God bless us. It is a wonderful occasion for a big family dinner, and if they know good food is waiting at home, maybe the wandering family members will come home and eat!

Family Dinner (for 10)

Cream of Pea Soup
Corned Beef and Cabbage Deluxe
Potatoes O'Brien
Irish Soda Bread
Shamrock Pie   Irish Coffee

Cream of Pea Soup

The difference between this soup and other pea soup is that this one is made from fresh peas or frozen green tiny peas, not the dried ones. It makes a big difference, and the soup is a lovely bright color.

**2 pounds fresh green peas or 2 packages (10 oz. each)
    frozen tiny peas in butter sauce
2 scallions, green part and all
2 tablespoons butter (if using fresh peas)
3 tablespoons flour
6 cups chicken broth or 6 chicken bouillon cubes
    dissolved in 6 cups hot water
Salt and pepper
Croutons**

Shell green peas, rinse, and set aside. If you are using frozen peas, let them thaw completely.

Clean and finely chop the scallions. If you are using fresh peas, melt butter in a large heavy soup pot and cook scallions until limp. If you are using frozen peas in butter sauce, drain the butter sauce into the soup pot and cook scallions in it.

Add flour to soup pot and stir to blend and make a smooth paste. Add a little more butter if necessary. Then add the chicken broth and cook and stir until all the flour mixture is smoothly incorporated. Add fresh peas and simmer 30 minutes.

If you are using frozen peas, let broth and flour mixture cook until smooth, stirring often, and until the flour smells cooked, about 5 minutes. Then add the peas and just heat them through.

Put the hot soup into the blender container—you will need to do this in several batches—and process until smooth and thick. Reheat gently. Taste and add salt and pepper if necessary. Serve garnished with croutons.

Hint: You could add a couple of tablespoons medium-dry sherry when you reheat the soup—very good but not really necessary. You could also cook some carrots, maybe two, in the soup. Again, nice, but not necessary.

Corned Beef and Cabbage Deluxe

This wonderful dish has had a bad press for years, usually because so many of us remember it with the cabbage cooked almost beyond recognition and certainly beyond palatability. This need not be so. It is in fact easier to do it right than to mess it up.

5 pounds lean corned beef in one piece
3 bay leaves
5 whole peppercorns
2 medium-sized heads green cabbage

Rinse the corned beef and put it in a large heavy pot with a tight lid with bay leaves, peppercorns, and water to generously cover the meat. Bring the liquid to a fast simmer over medium heat; do not let it boil; too much heat will make the beef gray and stringy. Reduce heat so that liquid barely simmers and cover the pot. Cook the beef for about 2½ hours (30 minutes per pound), until it is very tender when pierced with a fork or sharp knife.

When meat is done, take it out of the liquid and refrigerate, tightly wrapped. Refrigerate the liquid also. Do all this well ahead of serving time.

When you're ready to serve the meal, gently reheat the meat in simmering broth.

While meat heats, prepare cabbage. Remove wilted or damaged leaves and trim core flush with head. Do not remove core—it helps hold the cabbage together while it cooks. Cut cabbage into 2-inch wedges.

When the meat is hot, transfer it to a platter. Bring the cooking broth to a very mild boil, add the cabbage wedges, reduce heat so it barely simmers, and cover the pot. Check often. At the first hint of the smell of cooked cabbage—sooner if the cabbage is tender when pierced with a knife—turn off the heat and remove the cabbage with a slotted spoon. Keep warm.

While the cabbage cooks, thinly slice the meat across the grain at an angle.

The traditional potatoes with corned beef and cabbage are whole potatoes peeled and cooked in the broth. They are very good, too. If you want something a little more festive for this holiday meal, try Potatoes O'Brien.

Potatoes O'Brien

10 large potatoes, peeled and cut in 1-inch chunks
4 tablespoons butter
  Milk or light cream
  Salt and pepper
1 cup finely chopped parsley
½ cup finely chopped scallion, green part and all

Cook the potatoes in lightly salted boiling water until very tender, 20 to 30 minutes. Drain, reserving some of the potato water. Mash with butter and enough potato water and milk to make light, fluffy mashed potatoes. Taste and add salt and pepper if you wish. Add green stuff and mix.

Irish Soda Bread

    4 cups unbleached flour
    3 tablespoons sugar
    1 tablespoon baking powder
    1 teaspoon salt
    ¾ teaspoon baking soda
    6 tablespoons butter or margarine
1½ cups raisins
    1 tablespoon caraway seeds
    2 eggs
1½ cups buttermilk

Heat oven to 350°F. Grease a 2-quart casserole (the traditional shape is round).

In a large bowl, mix flour, sugar, baking powder, salt, and baking soda. Cut in the butter with a pastry blender or two knives until the mixture resembles coarse crumbs. Stir in raisins and caraway seeds.

In a medium-size bowl, beat the eggs lightly with a fork. Remove and reserve 1 tablespoon of the beaten egg.

Mix buttermilk into the bulk of the eggs and stir into the flour mixture just until the flour is moistened. The dough will be sticky. Turn dough out onto a well-floured board and, with floured hands, knead it about 10 strokes.

Shape dough into a ball and place in casserole. On the top cut a 4-inch cross about ¼ inch deep. Brush top of loaf with reserved beaten egg.

Bake about 1 hour and 20 minutes, or until a cake tester or toothpick comes out clean. Cool in casserole on a wire rack for 10 minutes, then remove bread from casserole and cool completely on the rack.

Shamrock Pie

You will recognize this recipe as Key Lime Pie under other circumstances. It is good and tastes fresh after this meal, and it is a suitable color for Saint Patrick's Day. If you feel the color is not intense enough, you can help it along with a little food coloring.

It used to be possible to make this pie without the gelatin, but a reformulation of condensed milk has made it necessary to stiffen up the mixture.

1 can (8 to 10 oz.) sweetened condensed milk
½ cup freshly squeezed lime juice (don't cheat)
  Grated rind of 1 lime
1 envelope unflavored gelatin
3 eggs
1 baked piecrust (page 115)

Mix condensed milk, lime juice, and lime rind.

Soften the gelatin in 2 tablespoons cold water. Heat until gelatin is completely melted and no granules show on the back of a spoon when it is stirred. The microwave for 30 seconds or a little more works very well. Add melted gelatin to milk mixture.

Lightly beat eggs and mix into milk. Pour filling into the baked piecrust and let set in the refrigerator several hours or overnight until the filling is firmly jelled.

Hints: If the members of your family are big dessert eaters, make two pies. It is easier to mix the amounts for them one at a time, however.

If you want to cut back a little on calories, you could serve the filling in small bowls and call it Shamrock Pudding. It hardly seems worth the effort for the savings accrued, though. Or maybe your family just doesn't like piecrust!

For this whole meal, beer seems like the ideal beverage. Coffee with the pie, of course—Irish coffee if you like it.

Irish Coffee

Fresh, hot, strong coffee
2 tablespoons Irish whiskey for each cup
Sugar (optional)
Heavy cream

Make the coffee the way you usually do. Pour it into cups—the little glasses get too hot to hold and the elegant glass cups have a bad habit of coming apart. Add whiskey to coffee. Sweeten with sugar if you like it. Float cream on the top of each cup by very carefully pouring it from a small pitcher over the back of a spoon that barely touches the surface of the coffee.

Hints: While it is true that Irish coffee can be fairly powerful, a lot of the alcohol evaporates when the whiskey hits the hot coffee. Keep this information to yourself.

You may have some leftover corned beef from your holiday meal. You certainly hope so. The corned beef makes sandwiches to weep over, much better than the corned beef you buy. If there is quite a lot, you are in the way of being able to make a New England Boiled Dinner. Just cook potatoes, beets, more cabbage, and small whole onions separately in the reserved broth or lightly salted water. Unite them with sliced corned beef in soup bowls with some broth.

If you have a significant amount of potatoes left over, transform them into potato soup. You can serve it up to three or four days later, but it tastes much better if you actually make it while you put the food away and scrape the dishes from your Saint Patrick's day meal. Just dilute Potatoes O'Brien with milk and chicken broth to make a fairly thick soup. Store tightly covered in the refrigerator until ready to serve.

If there is much cabbage left, reheat it, chop it up, and mix with a fresh batch of hot mashed potatoes or reheated leftover Potatoes O'Brien. Pile the mixture into a serving dish drizzle melted butter on top. You have now made Colcannon. Traditionally, it is served on Allhallows Eve—Halloween to us—with charms buried inside: a ring, a new penny, a thimble, and a button. The people who find the charms can expect to be married within the year, get rich, become a spinster or a bachelor respectively. If you have the charms and want to use them, by all means alert your guests to the existence of the charms. One of my aunts baked her family charms in the Christmas pudding without warning the first year she was with us. She used twelve charms—but only saw six of them again. How were we to know?

4

Passover

PASSOVER IS A WONDERFULLY HAPPY HOLIDAY RICH IN HIS-
tory and food tradition. Many families have passed recipes
down for generations. If you would like some additional ideas,
perhaps to establish a tradition of your own, you'll find some
suggestions in this chapter.

As usual, for a successful holiday meal, plan ahead, get the
shopping done early, and do as much cooking ahead of time
as you can. There are also special things to be done for Passover. Get out your holiday dishes; do a thorough houseclean-
ing. Enlist any children to help—it is definitely part of their
learning experience, and it can be a lot of fun, too. The secret
of success is to spread the work around and be generous with
rewards so that nobody gets exhausted and cross. The younger
the children, the shorter the work sessions should be.

Order your main supplies early. There is a positive run on
beautiful briskets and good-size roasting chickens and capons
around the holiday. If you have difficulty finding matzos for
Passover, start your search early. Maybe your grocer will order
some for you even if the store doesn't usually stock them.

Braised Brisket of Beef Seder

Now all organized and serene, put out your best linen and
your most beautiful tableware. Arrange spring flowers and polish up the good candlesticks. Get some rest and prepare to
enjoy this most joyous celebration.

Please note that keeping "kosher for Passover" requires
careful observance of Jewish dietary laws. If you have any
questions about the ingredients or preparation of the food in
these recipes, consult a rabbi.

Braised Brisket of Beef Seder (for 12)

Chicken Soup with Matzo Dumplings
Braised Brisket with Gravy and Horseradish
Potato Pancakes   Glazed Carrots and Parsnips
Spring Salad
Fruit Compote

Chicken Soup with Matzo Dumplings

Good chicken stock is the base of good matzo soup. The stock really must be made at least a day or two in advance so that the fat can be removed.

1 stewing chicken (about 5 lb.), including giblets and cleaned feet, cut into pieces
4 quarts water
5 celery stalks, roughly chopped
5 carrots, roughly chopped
1 large onion, halved and stuck with 1 whole clove
1 garlic clove, halved
Parsley sprigs
2 bay leaves
5 or 6 peppercorns
Salt

Put the chicken in a really big, heavy pot. Cover with 4 quarts water and bring to a boil. Skim off any scum (the fluffy stuff) that rises as the soup begins to cook. Reduce heat so that the water barely simmers.

Add vegetables, spices, and salt to taste. Partially cover and let soup simmer until the chicken is very tender, 2 to 3 hours.

Let soup pot cool enough to handle. Strain the broth into a very large container; cool, cover tightly, and refrigerate at least overnight so that fat will rise and solidify. When it does, remove and discard it. Put the poached chicken away—it will make wonderful chicken salad. Discard the giblets and the vegetables; they have given their all.

At least a few hours before you plan to serve the soup, make the matzo dumplings.

Matzo Dumplings

    6 eggs
    6 tablespoons melted chicken fat
    ⅛ teaspoon ground nutmeg (optional)
      Freshly ground pepper (optional)
    ¼ cup water
      Salt
    1¼ cups (approx.) matzo meal
      Fresh parsley or dill, minced (optional)

In a large bowl, beat the eggs until they are fluffy. Add chicken fat, spices, water, and salt to taste. Mix well.

Carefully stir in enough of the matzo meal to form a stiff dough, adding more meal if necessary. Tightly cover dough and refrigerate until 45 minutes before finishing soup, at least an hour (longer is better).

To finish soup, bring the defatted broth to a boil in a large pot. A pan that is fairly shallow is easier to work with than a narrow deep pot.

Take matzo dough out of the refrigerator. Moisten hands with cold water, and form dough into 1- to 1½-inch balls. Drop the balls into boiling soup.

Adjust heat so that broth boils gently but steadily and cook matzo dumplings about 30 minutes. They should be firm but tender. Carefully ladle the soup and matzo balls into warmed soup bowls. Garnish with a little finely minced parsley or fresh dill if you would like a touch of color.

Hints: Keep in mind when finishing the soup that it takes 12 or so cups of cold liquid some time to come to a boil and factor that into your planning.

If your market does not carry rendered chicken fat, you can make your own. Save and freeze the fat that you remove from roasting chickens as you use them. When you have accumulated enough to make it worthwhile, let the fat thaw, cut it into 1-inch pieces, and put them in the top of a double boiler. Cook over simmering water until all the fat is rendered. Strain into a storage container with a tight lid and store in the refrigerator until needed. This method is a lot easier and safer than rendering fat over direct heat. The cracklings never burn, and the fat never catches fire!

Braised Brisket with Gravy and Horseradish

For 12 people, you will need to make this recipe twice, about 5 pound of beef in all. It is easier to do it in 2 pots. For each batch, you will need:

2 first cut briskets of beef (2½ lbs.)
Soy sauce or gravy flavoring
2 large onions, sliced
2 garlic cloves, peeled and chopped
Salt and pepper
Fresh horseradish

The day before you plan to serve it, brush the brisket with soy sauce or gravy flavoring and let it stand at room temperature while you prepare the onions and garlic. Put on a kettle of water to boil.

In a large heavy pot with a lid, gently brown the brisket over medium heat. Take your time. Then add onions and garlic. Add boiling water to cover the meat entirely. Adjust the heat so that the water barely simmers. Partially cover the pot and simmer the meat for about 3½ hours, until it is very tender. The secret here is very *slow* cooking.

When the meat is tender, let it cool in the broth, then wrap tightly and store in the refrigerator. If you want thin gravy (almost beef broth), strain the cooking liquid and discard the onions and garlic. Let broth cool, then refrigerate. Remove all the fat that rises to the top. If you would like thick gravy, leave onions and garlic in. Remove fat, and process in a blender until smooth (you may need to do it in several batches). In either case, taste the broth and season with salt and pepper.

To serve, very gently reheat the meat in a 200°F. oven, just until it is hot through. Slice very thin diagonally across the grain. Serve with gravy and fresh horseradish.

Beet Horseradish

You can usually find prepared beet horseradish in the dairy case in supermarkets, but it will be much better (and hotter) if you make it fresh. It's easy, too. If you are using a food processor, be cautious. You want to leave a little texture.

1½ cups finely grated fresh horseradish
½ cup grated raw beet
½ cup (approx.) white vinegar substitute
1 teaspoon salt (approx.)
1 teaspoon sugar (approx.)
   Ice water

Grate the horseradish and beet. If you do it by hand, watch your knuckles. If you use a food processor, cut vegetables into fairly small pieces and pulse rather than start the processor. You want grated, not pureed.

Add vinegar substitute, salt, and sugar to taste. Add ice water, a teaspoon at a time, until you get the texture you want.

Put the horseradish in an attractive bowl and tightly cover. Refrige for at least an hour.

Hint: Vinegar, of course, is not Kosher for Passover, but there are special brand names that market substitutes for holiday use.

Potato Pancakes (Latkes)

These are the real thing, better than we deserve. The food processor has taken a lot of the anguish out of making them. Usually associated with Chanukah, latkes are also a popular Passover treat.

6 fairly large potatoes, peeled
1 large onion, cut up roughly
1 egg
½ cup matzo meal
1 teaspoon salt
½ teaspoon freshly ground pepper
   Vegetable oil

Process potatoes and onion with the grating disk of a food processor. If you do this by hand, take care; use the side of the grater with the big holes. Also, work with onion halves, not pieces.

Mix potatoes and onion with egg, matzo meal, salt, and pepper.

Heat a griddle or very large skillet. Add about ⅛ inch vegetable oil. Drop pancake batter onto griddle by ¼ cupfuls; use a ¼-cup measuring cup to keep pancakes uniform. Fry about 2 minutes on each side, just until golden brown. Add oil to griddle as necessary.

When pancakes are done, drain on paper towels. Keep warm in a very slow oven.

Hint: This recipe makes 24 pancakes. You can make them far in advance and freeze them. Reheat the latkes in a 350°F. oven for 10 or 15 minutes.

It is probably a good idea to keep a supply of latkes in the freezer. They turn a ho-hum meal into something special and are also very good with sour cream and applesauce as a sort of superdeluxe snack.

Glazed Carrots and Parsnips

 6 **large parsnips**
 6 **large carrots**
   Salt
½ **cup orange marmalade**
 2 **tablespoons lemon juice**

Scrub parsnips and carrots and cut in half lengthwise, then in quarters; you may want to use smaller long slices, depending on the size of the vegetables. Cover parsnips with lightly salted water in a large saucepan and bring to a boil. Cook 10 minutes; then add the carrots. Add more boiling water if necessary. Cook the vegetables until they are very tender but not falling apart.

While vegetables cook, melt the marmalade and thin it with the lemon juice. When vegetables are tender, carefully drain them and pour the sweet-sour glaze over them. Cover the pan and gently shake to coat all surfaces. Leave in pan, partially covered, until you're ready to serve the meal. The glaze will just get nicer. Give the pan another good shake before serving.

Spring Salad

2 heads Boston lettuce
1 small bunch watercress
2 avocados
2 tablespoons lemon juice
3 or 4 scallions, green parts and all

Wash and trim lettuce and watercress. Wrap in a towel and refrigerate.

Peel avocados and cut into thin lengthwise slices. Sprinkle with lemon juice. Wrap tightly and refrigerate.

Clean and slice scallions.

At serving time tear greens into bite-size pieces and arrange avocados and scallions on top of them. Drizzle Orange Dressing over the salad. Toss at the table just before serving.

Orange Dressing

½ cup orange juice
¼ cup lemon juice
½ cup vegetable oil
Salt and freshly ground pepper

Put all ingredients into a screw-top jar and shake until creamy.

Fruit Compote

Start with a package of mixed dried fruits, and then add to it what your family likes best. We go for the apricots. The proportions given here are just suggestions.

1 box (8 oz.) mixed dried fruits
1 package (8 oz.) dried apricots
1 package (16 oz.) *pitted* **prunes**
   Sugar
2 cinnamon sticks
¼ cup orange juice
2 tablespoons grated orange rind
   Shredded coconut

Make sure all the mixed dried fruits have been pitted. Soak all the fruit for at least 30 minutes in hot tap water to cover by 1 inch. If all the water is absorbed, add a little more.

Heat sugar, cinnamon sticks, and orange juice in a small saucepan. Drain the fruit, if necessary, and add the soaking liquid to the orange juice. Pour the orange juice mixture over the fruit, stir well, and let stand at room temperature for at least an hour.

Put the compote in a serving dish, cover tightly, and chill in the refrigerator until ready to serve. Sprinkle coconut over the top of fruits.

Hint: This compote is very good with macaroons. You can buy them or make them, using the recipe that follows.

Macaroons

1 tablespoon plus 1 teaspoon matzo cake meal
1 pound shredded coconut
4 cups confectioners' sugar
2 lemon grated rinds
5 egg whites

Combine all ingredients except egg whites and blend well.
Beat egg whites to stiff but not dry peaks and fold into
batter.

Heat oven to 300°F. Dust a cookie sheet generously with
cake meal and drop macaroons from a teaspoon, allowing 1
inch between them. Bake for 15 minutes.

Increase heat to 350°F. and continue baking 10 to 15
minutes, until macaroons are browned. Cool on cookie sheet
on a rack.

Hints: The easiest way to grate the rind of citrus fruits is to
do it while the fruit is whole. You can always juice it later.

Egg whites beat to better volume and work better in recipes
if they are at room temperature when beaten.

Roast Chicken Seder

Roast Chicken Seder (for 12)

Chilled Melon
Gefilte Fish in Fish Aspic
Lime Roast Chicken
Potato Kugel   Braised Endive
Cucumber Salad
Passover Sponge Cake with Lemon Glaze

Gefilte Fish in Fish Aspic

It takes quite a while to make gefilte fish, but the result really is worth the trouble. The good news is that this dish can (and must) be made ahead of time. It keeps quite happily for several days in the refrigerator.

5½ **pounds assorted freshwater fish such as whitefish, pike, carp**
  6 **medium-size onions**
  4 **carrots**
  2 **quarts water**
  2 **celery stalks**
  4 **eggs, beaten**
  1 **cup ice water**
 ½ **cup matzo meal**
  1 **teaspoon sugar (optional)**
  3 **teaspoons salt**
  2 **teaspoons white pepper**
    Beet horseradish (optional)

Have the fish filleted and keep the heads, skin, and bones; you will need them for the stock.

Slice 3 of the onions and 2 of the carrots. Line the bottom of a heavy 3-quart pot with the vegetables. Add fish heads, skin, and bones. Add 2 quarts water and bring to a boil. Cook at a fast simmer while preparing gefilte fish.

Grind the fish fillets with the remaining 3 onions and 2 carrots and the celery. A food processor is definitely the tool to use here; if you don't have one, use a food mill. Add the remaining ingredients to the processor and process to a fine paste, or put the ground mixture in a chopping bowl, add remaining ingredients gradually, and chop to a very fine paste. Refrigerate the mixture for 15 or 20 minutes for easier handling.

When fish mixture is thoroughly chilled, shape it into 2-inch balls or 1½ × 3-inch quenelles. Lower the balls or quenelles gently into simmering fish stock, cover, and simmer slowly 1½ hours. Remove cover for the last 30 minutes of cooking. Add more water if necessary to keep fish covered. Let cool in pot.

When the pot is cool, lift out fish balls or quenelles with a slotted spoon and place in one layer in a deep platter. Strain the fish stock and pour it over the fish. Garnish with the sliced carrots from the stock. Cover tightly and refrigerate until ready to serve. Serve with Beet Horseradish (page 53) if you like—very pretty.

Hints: Fish stock should jell, but it may not be a firm aspic. If you would like it stiffer, ask your fish monger for extra bones.

If you don't have a chopping bowl, now is the time to get one. You'll find it useful for many processes. Buy a larger bowl than you think you'll need; the little ones are only an annoyance unless you are chopping three sprigs of parsley.

Gourmet chefs make quenelles by dipping a serving spoon in ice water, then taking a spoonful of the fish mixture and slipping it delicately off the inverted spoon with another spoon or a spatula. The result: neat and uniform quenelles. You might like to try this method, but hands moistened in ice water also work very well.

Lime Roast Chicken

2 roasting chickens (5 lb. each)
3 limes
   Salt
   Freshly ground pepper
½ cup chicken stock or dry white wine

Heat oven to 450°F. Wash and dry chickens thoroughly inside and out. Put wings behind back and tie legs together. Reserve giblets for another use.

Place the chickens on a rack over a roasting pan. Squeeze the juice of 1½ limes over each chicken (use more if you wish). Sprinkle the chickens lightly with salt and generously with pepper.

Roast the chickens for 15 minutes. Reduce oven heat to 325°F. and continue cooking for another 1 hour and 45 minutes. Baste with pan juices or more lime juice about every 20 minutes. The chickens are done when juices from the thigh run clear instead of pink and the legs move easily.

Transfer chickens to serving platter. Drain cooking juices and discard as much fat as possible. Return the juices to the roasting pan and heat gently. Stir to get up all the brown bits from the bottom of the pan. Add about ½ cup chicken stock or wine to sauce and serve hot with chicken.

Potato Kugel

- **6 large raw potatoes, peeled**
- **6 eggs**
- **6 tablespoons chicken fat**
- **2 large onions, finely chopped**
- **1½ cups matzo meal**
- **1 teaspoon salt**

Grate the potatoes into ice water and set aside.

In a large bowl, beat the eggs. In a large heavy skillet heat the chicken fat, add the onions, and sauté until golden.

Very thoroughly drain the potatoes and add them to the eggs. Transfer the sautéed onions to potato mixture with a slotted spoon; reserve the chicken fat they were cooked in. Add the matzo meal and salt to the potato mixture and mix well.

Grease a 3-quart baking dish with the reserved chicken fat. Turn the potato mixture into the baking dish. Bake in a 325°F. over (right along with the chicken) for about 1¼ hours.

Braised Endive

Expensive, yes. Delicious, yes. Festive, certainly. Worth every penny!

- **24 small heads endive**
- **4 tablespoons melted chicken fat**
  - **Salt and pepper**
- **1 tablespoon finely minced fresh dill**
- **1 tablespoon finely minced parsley**
  - **Dash nutmeg**
- **2 cups chicken broth (approx.)**

Clean endive, remove wilted leaves, and cut off woody root end. If heads are very small, leave them whole. Cut larger heads in half lengthwise.

In a flat heatproof, ovenproof dish with a lid, sauté the endive in the chicken fat until it is *very* lightly browned. Treat it gently; you don't want it to come apart. Add salt and pepper to taste and sprinkle with the dill, parsley, and nutmeg. Add enough chicken broth to the pan to barely cover the endive.

Cover and braise in a 325°F. oven for 1½ hours. Uncover for the last ½ hour. Add a little more broth if necessary; most of it should cook away during the braising process. Baste endive with remaining pan juices and serve in baking dish.

Cucumber Salad

 6 **cucumbers**
 Salt
 ½ **cup vinegar substitute**
2½ **tablespoons sugar**
 2 **teaspoons salt**
 Freshly ground pepper
 ¼ **cup water**
 3 **scallions, sliced thin, green part and all**
 Boston lettuce or other greens (optional)

Thinly slice the cucumbers. Some varieties of cucumber have thinner skins and smaller seeds. If they are available at your market, use them in this recipe—no need to peel. Put them in a bowl and salt well. Let stand 15 minutes; drain and rinse with cold water. Pat dry.

In a small saucepan combine vinegar substitute, sugar, the 2 teaspoons salt, and pepper to taste with the ¼ cup water. Mix well and bring to a boil. Pour over cucumbers. Sprinkle with scallions.

Chill the salad at least 3 hours. Serve in Boston lettuce cups, if you wish, or over other salad greens.

Passover Sponge Cake with Lemon Glaze

½ cup matzo cake meal
½ cup potato starch
10 egg yolks
1 teaspoon grated orange rind
3 tablespoons orange juice
1 teaspoon grated lemon rind
1 tablespoon lemon juice
1 teaspoon vanilla extract
½ teaspoon almond extract
10 egg whites
1 cup sugar

Sift matzo meal and potato starch together 3 times; set aside.

Beat egg yolks until stiff—definitely a job for an electric mixer. Stir in the orange rind and juice, the lemon rind and juice, and the vanilla and almond extracts.

Beat the egg whites until they form soft peaks. Continue beating as you add the sugar, 1 tablespoon at a time.

Very gently fold egg yolk mixture into egg whites, using as few strokes as possible.

Lightly sprinkle the matzo meal and potato starch mixture over eggs and fold in with as few strokes as possible. It is all right if there are some white flecks left.

Heat oven to 325°F. Pour the cake batter into an ungreased 10-inch tube pan and bake 50 to 60 minutes, until a cake tester comes out clean. When cake is done, remove from oven, invert pan, and let cool completely. The cake will usually fall out by itself; if not, use a very thin knife to loosen the sides and around the tube.

Lemon Glaze

1 **egg yolk**
½ **cup lemon juice**
1 **cup confectioners' sugar**
1 **lemon rind, grated**
1 **teaspoon vegetable shortening**

Mix all ingredients except the shortening. Bring to a boil in a small saucepan and cook, stirring constantly, until mixture has thickened.

Remove pan from heat. Add shortening and beat to mix well.

Let cool until warm. Pour on top of sponge cake and let any extra glaze drizzle down the sides.

Hints: Sponge cake tastes better if it is made the day before it is to be used or even earlier. If you want to glaze it right before serving, fine, but you can do that in advance, too.

If your cake breaks or a piece of the bottom doesn't come out with the rest of the cake, patch it together with glaze. No one will ever know.

5

⊛⊛⊛⊛⊛⊛⊛⊛⊛⊛

Easter

EASTER IS THE FIRST TASTE OF SPRING FOR MANY OF US. A TO-
tally joyous holiday, the celebration of the return to life from
death, the rebirth of flowers and green things, all the spring
festivals rolled into one.

Food traditions abound, but they are not binding. Some families attend midnight mass on Easter Eve, and in some cultures
it is traditional to have a big dinner afterward. If that is a bit
late for you, you could have an earlier supper. The French eat
omelets Easter morning, and so can you. A big Easter dinner
is a great time for families and friends to get together.

The usual holiday preparations apply to Easter, too, but a
couple of things need special consideration. For instance, eggs.
Usually those of us who buy eggs at the supermarket do not
have to be concerned that they are too fresh. On the contrary!
But the demand is so great around Easter and Passover that
the supply of eggs tends to turn over very, very fast. It is next
to impossible to peel a very fresh hard-boiled egg, and very
fresh egg whites do not beat well. There goes the soufflé.

Get your shopping done as soon as is practical.

1. Up to two weeks before Easter, buy all of the eggs you
    will need for the holiday. Remember that there will be
    Easter eggs for the kids to dye or for you to decorate for
    lovely centerpieces; the eggs for the Russian Easter Eggs;
    eggs for Hollandaise sauce and meringue shells; and eggs
    for family breakfasts as usual. Put eggs in the refrigerator
    and let them age.

65

2. At least a week before Easter:

   Hard-boil the eggs for Russian Easter Eggs.

   Order your crown roast of lamb from the butcher and shop for the size canned ham you need. Both these items get scarce close to Easter.

   Make sure holiday linens are in order.

   Check your candle supply.

   Order flowers and arrange for delivery.

   Does your silver need polishing? Do it now.

3. Early in the week before Easter:

   Make meringue shells. When they are completely cool, store in an airtight container.

   Dye those Easter eggs. Modern Easter egg dyes make the job less messy and spills temporary. Cover everything with newspapers and let the kids have at it. You can do your own for decoration at a quiet time.

   Peel the hard-boiled eggs you made for Russian Easter Eggs. Gently crack the chilled eggs all over and soak in cold water for 10 minutes. The peels should come off easily. You might add a teaspoon of salt to the soaking water. You might also want to hard-boil some spares in case the worst happens.

   Set Russian Easter Eggs in their pickling solutions to steep. Do the supermarket shopping.

4. The day before Easter:

   Pick up the crown roast.

Crown Roast of Lamb Dinner

Either of the two menus in this chapter would be suitable for a big Easter Eve dinner after midnight church. If your appetite after midnight does not run to so much food, consider serving omelets, Eggs Benedict (but not if you're having Hollandaise sauce the next day), Turkey Lasagne (page 26), or Seafood Fondue (page 29).

> Crown Roast of Lamb Dinner (for 12)
>
> Cold Cream of Cucumber Soup
> Crown Roast of Lamb with Bulgur Wheat Stuffing
> Roast Potatoes and Onions
> Asparagus with Hollandaise Sauce
> Wilted Lettuce and Scallion Salad
> Meringue Shells with Strawberries

Cold Cream of Cucumber Soup

You will need to make two batches of this soup.

2 chicken bouillon cubes
3 cups yogurt
4 cucumbers cut in chunks
2 peeled garlic cloves
2 scallions, green part and all, sliced roughly
½ bunch fresh dill
**   Parsley sprigs**
**   Salt**

Put everything in the blender container and process until you don't hear any loud clonking sounds; that will mean the bouillon cubes are completely dissolved. Keep the soup very cold until you're ready to serve it. Make two batches for 12 diners.

Hint: If your blender is not powerful enough to completely break up the cucumber seeds, you may want to remove them for a smoother soup.

Crown Roast of Lamb with Bulgur Wheat Stuffing

Ask your butcher to prepare a crown roast, and be sure to say how many people you are feeding. This is a dish for a big group, since it is almost impossible to make a crown roast with fewer than 16 or 18 chops. You'll need 18 to 20 chops for twelve people—some will eat more than one serving.

1 crown roast of lamb (18 to 20 chops)
1 large garlic clove
Flour
Salt and pepper

Heat oven to 350°F.

Wipe meat all over with slightly damp paper towels. Peel the garlic clove, cut it in half, and rub every surface of the roast, bones and all, with the garlic pieces.

Mix flour with salt and pepper. Rub the meat well with it, inside and out.

Put the roast in a pan, bare bone tips up, and bake 1 hour for very rare lamb, up to 1½ hours for well done. Remove from oven and let stand at least 10 minutes before carving.

While roast cooks, make stuffing.

Bulgur Wheat Stuffing

1½ cup bulgur wheat
3 cups water or broth
1 medium-size onion, finely chopped
2 celery stalks, finely chopped
3 tablespoons chopped parsley
3 tablespoons butter
1 teaspoon thyme
1 teaspoon rosemary
2 teaspoons grated lemon peel
Parsley sprigs (optional)
Cherry tomatoes (optional)

Rinse bulgur wheat in a sieve and drain while water or broth comes to a boil. Add wheat to liquid gradually, reduce heat so pot barely simmers, and cover tightly. Cook on lowest possible heat for about 20 minutes, until all liquid is absorbed.

Sauté the onion, celery, and parsley in butter until the onion is translucent and the celery is still a little crisp.

Add vegetables and any remaining butter to the bulgur wheat. Stir in spices and lemon peel. Taste the mixture and add salt and pepper if desired.

Pile stuffing into the center of the crown roast. Garnish with parsley or cherry tomatoes if you like.

Hints: Look for bulgur at a health food store or one that sells Middle Eastern groceries if your supermarket doesn't stock it.

You can decorate the ends of the chop bones with cherry tomatoes or with the paper frills available in stationery stores and gourmet food outlets. You can also make your own: Take a piece of paper twice as wide as you wish your frills to be and long enough to go around the bone tips easily. Fold the paper lengthwise. Cut about halfway through the folded edge of the paper every ¹⁄₁₆ inch. Open the frill and fold the other way. Secure with transparent tape. Voilà! Frills. You can make larger frills for a ham or leg of lamb bone using the same method.

Roast Potatoes and Onions

12 or more medium-size baking potatoes
12 or more plain yellow onions about the same size as the potatoes

Peel the potatoes or leave the skin on, as you prefer.

Scruff the onions with your hands to get off just the dry papery leaves that will come away easily.

Arrange potatoes around the crown roast or on a separate pan or cookie sheet. Put the onions in a separate pan with sides (they sometimes give up enough liquid to make roasting on a cookie sheet messy). Bake in oven with the crown roast, same time, same temperature; if the potatoes need a little more cooking, you can leave them in the oven while the roast rests before it is carved.

Hint: Roast onions, by themselves, are perfectly delicious with many meats. And they couldn't be easier. Serve them with butter, salt, and pepper, just like the potatoes.

Asparagus with Hollandaise Sauce

4 pounds fresh asparagus (approx.)
2 tablespoons water
Hollandaise Sauce

Rinse asparagus and break off woody ends of the stalks. Steam until tender but still crisp.

Make Hollandaise Sauce.

Hollandaise Sauce

12 egg yolks
3 tablespoons cold water
¼ cup lemon juice (approx.), strained
¾ pound (3 sticks) butter cut into ¼-inch slices

In the top of a double boiler over barely simmering water that does not touch the bottom of the upper pan, beat egg yolks and cold water to mix very well. A whisk is the best tool for this job.

Beat lemon juice into egg yolks and begin adding butter, a few slices at a time. Continue beating all the time. By the time all the butter has been incorporated, the sauce will be thick and smooth. Taste the sauce and add salt.

Immediately take the upper part of the double boiler off the bottom pan and replace the simmering water with cold water. Put sauce over cold water to stop the cooking process. Cover and set aside until ready to serve.

If you wish to reheat the sauce, do so *very* gently over hot but not simmering water.

Hint: Hollandaise Sauce has the reputation of being hard to make. It is not. You have to make sure that the water is kept below boiling and that it doesn't touch the bottom of the top pan. The sauce will need your full attention, but for only a short time.

You may have read that Hollandaise Sauce cannot be successfully reheated. No again. Just do it gently.

If the worst happens and your sauce starts to curdle, remove it from the heat *immediately* and vigorously beat in 1 or 2 tablespoons very hot water.

Wilted Lettuce and Scallion Salad

3 slices bacon
⅓ cup cider vinegar
⅓ cup water

Salt and pepper
Sugar (optional)
36 **leaves leaf lettuce, all green or red-tipped, cleaned**
    and torn into bite-size pieces
 6 **scallions, green parts and all, thinly sliced**

Fry the bacon in a heavy skillet until very crisp but not scorched. Drain bacon on paper towels.

Add vinegar and water to the hot bacon fat. Taste for salt (you may not need any, since the bacon is salty) and pepper. You might want to add a pinch of sugar if the vinegar is very tart.

Place the lettuce and onions in a large salad bowl. Just before serving pour the hot dressing over the lettuce. Crumble the bacon and add it to the salad bowl if you like.

Hints: This salad used to be the very first dish from the garden in springtime. Now leaf lettuce and scallions are available year round, but it is still a salad associated in many minds with the coming of warmer weather and the joy of the season.

Be careful when you add the liquid to the hot fat. It spits.

Meringue Shells with Strawberries

You really need to make the meringue shells well ahead of time. They are easy, but they must dry out in a very, very slow oven for an extended time. So start early.

12 **egg whites at room temperature**
¼ **teaspoon salt**
½ **teaspoon cream of tartar**
2½ **cups sugar**
 2 **teaspoons vanilla extract**

Beat egg whites until they are thoroughly mixed and foamy. Add salt and cream of tartar and beat to dissolve them.

Add sugar, 2 tablespoons at a time. Continue beating until stiff glossy peaks form. Do not overbeat or the egg whites will be dry and will not maintain their shape well.

Add vanilla and mix well.

Cover cookie sheets with brown paper or wax paper. Form 12 meringue shells with a cake-decorating bag or (easier) with a large spoon. Gently press the back of the spoon into the meringue to form a small depression in each meringue shell.

Dry the meringues out in the oven at 200°F. for about an hour. The finished shells should be firm but still white. To maintain the very low oven temperature, you may need to prop the door open slightly with a wooden clothespin or a wooden spoon handle.

Gently remove the meringue shells from the paper while they are still warm. Let them cool completely on a rack. Store at room temperature in airtight containers.

Strawberries

3 pints fresh strawberries or 3 packages frozen strawberries (10 oz. each)
Sugar
Whipped cream or ice cream

Wash, hull, and slice all but 12 of the fresh berries. Add sugar to taste, about 1 cup. Cover and refrigerate.

If you are using frozen berries, simply let them thaw. Store in the refrigerator instead of the freezer. There is no need to add sugar.

To serve, spoon berries into meringue shells. Top with reserved whole berries, if you have them, and whipped cream or ice cream.

Hint: Add a tablespoon or two of a liqueur to the strawberries if you wish.

Ham en Croûte Dinner

Ham en Croûte Dinner (for 12)

Artichokes with Green Mayonnaise
Ham en Croûte
Russian Easter Eggs
New Potatoes   Green Beans and Baby Carrots
Dandelion Green Salad
Lemon Sherbet

Artichokes with Green Mayonnaise

12 medium-size artichokes
½ lemon
  Green Mayonnaise

Wash the artichokes and cut off stem and a few of the small bottom leaves. Cut off about ½ inch from the top of each choke. Trim the tip of each leaf with kitchen scissors or poultry shears.

Cook artichokes in lightly salted water with the half lemon until a fork goes easily into the bottom of the choke where the stem was cut off. Drain chokes very thoroughly upside down. When they are completely cool, refrigerate them. Serve each person a whole artichoke to eat, pull the leaves off with your fingers and dip in green mayonnaise. Strip tender flesh from each leaf with your teeth.

Green Mayonnaise

If you love to make mayonnaise, by all means do. However, you can also use your regular brand, and it is a lot less work.

½ cup lemon juice, strained
½ cup parsley
½ cup fresh dill
½ cup chopped chives or the green part of scallions
 3 cups mayonnaise

Put the lemon juice, parsley, dill, and chives in the container of the blender and process until a fairly smooth puree is formed.

Mix puree with mayonnaise very thoroughly and refrigerate it, tightly covered. Serve in small bowls as a dip for the artichoke leaves.

Hint: We are often told to remove the center part of the artichoke before serving, but that is messy work. Just serve them whole; when guests run out of edible leaves, they are done, unless they want to take the fuzzy choke out and cut up and eat the artichoke bottoms.

Remember to provide someplace to put the inedible parts of

the artichoke leaves as they collect. Usually serving the artichokes on fairly large plates works fine.

Ham en Croûte

This main dish looks very festive, but it's not at all hard to
make. If you use packaged piecrust, it is a snap.

Piecrust dough for 2 pies (page 115)
1 canned ready-to-eat ham (approx. 8 lbs.)
Prepared mustard
¼ cup brown sugar
1 egg beaten with 1 tablespoon water

Roll the piecrust dough into a thin sheet large enough to
cover the top and sides of the ham. Set aside.

Heat the oven to 325°F.

Thoroughly drain the ham. Put it on a rack above a shallow
baking pan.

Mix enough prepared mustard with brown sugar to form a
thick paste. Rub it into the top and sides of the ham.

Drape the pie crust dough over the ham. Trim bottom edges
neatly and pinch and smooth dough so that it conforms to the
shape of the ham. Use the trimmings to decorate the top of
the ham. Tulip shapes are easy to cut out; roll thin strips of
dough to make the stems and use longer pieces to shape leaves.
Lilies of the valley are also attractive; they are just little inverted tulips on drooping curved stems. A bunch of grapes?
Whatever your imagination and talent run to. Brush finished
pastry all over with the egg beaten with water. Cut several
steam vents in the top of the crust.

Bake until the pastry shell is nicely browned. The ham only
needs to reach serving temperature, since it is fully cooked
already. Heating the ham and browning the pastry will take
about 40 minutes.

Russian Easter Eggs

12 hard-boiled eggs, peeled
2 cups white vinegar
1 cup water
2 teaspoons salt

2 **tablespoons sugar**
1 **tablespoon mixed pickling spices**
  Food coloring
  Cream cheese, softened or whipped
  Dandelion green salad

Peel eggs and store them, covered with water, in a covered container in the refrigerator until you are ready to color them.

In a saucepan combine all of the remaining ingredients except the food coloring. Bring this pickling solution to a simmer and keep it simmering for 5 minutes. Let cool and taste. Add more vinegar (strengths vary) or salt or sugar as needed.

Divide pickling solution among 3 or 4 large jars. Color each jar with several drops of food coloring. The more food coloring you use, the darker the hue of the eggs will be. Divide the eggs among the jars. The pickling solution should completely cover the eggs, and they should not be crowded. Cover the jars tightly and refrigerate. The eggs can and should marinate for at least 48 hours.

Before serving, drain the eggs and dry them carefully. Decorate with softened or whipped cream cheese using the smallest star tip of a cake decorating set. Make rosettes, ribbons, whatever strikes your fancy. Serve the eggs on a dandelion green salad with dressing spooned over them.

Hint: If you have pickle juice around, by all means use it to marinate the eggs. Nothing turns eggs a more beautiful red than pickled beet juice; other pickle juice can be tinted with food coloring.

New Potatoes

24 **very small new potatoes**
 4 **or 5 tablespoons butter**
 4 **tablespoons chopped fresh parsley**

Scrub potatoes well but do not peel. Steam in very little water until they are just tender; do not overcook.

If there is water left in the pan, drain it and return pan to heat. Add butter and stir gently to melt it and coat the potatoes. Toss in parsley and stir. If potatoes must stand before you serve them, remove from heat, cover pan with a kitchen towel, then put the lid on.

Green Beans and Baby Carrots

3 pounds fresh green beans
Tiny carrots, canned or frozen
Melted butter (optional)
Lemon juice (optional)

Steam the beans whole until they are crisp-tender. Do not overcook. Drain the beans well.

Gently heat canned baby carrots or cook frozen carrots as directed on the package.

Serve beans with carrots arranged around the outside of the platter. Drizzle with a little butter and lemon juice if you wish.

Hint: Canned baby carrots often taste sweeter than frozen ones.

Lemon Sherbet

This recipe makes 1 quart of sherbet. You will need to make 2 batches.

2 egg whites
½ cup sugar
1 cup corn syrup
2 cups milk
¾ cup lemon juice
Grated rind of ½ lemon

Beat egg whites until stiff but shiny peaks form. Add sugar a little at a time. Fold in other ingredients until very well mixed.

Pour into a freezer container and freeze until very firm, several hours or overnight. Put in a cold bowl and beat to break up lumps. Return to freezer and freeze until firm.

Hints: If you have an ice-cream freezer, use it.

The amount of sugar varies because some people want a sweeter dessert. This sherbet could be classed as a palate cleaner if only ¼ cup of sugar is used, as a dessert if ½ cup is used.

Lemon sherbet looks beautiful when served with sliced and sweetened fresh strawberries. It is also very good with thin, simple cookies.

6

Memorial Day

MEMORIAL DAY WEEKEND MARKS THE OFFICIAL BEGINNING OF the summer season for many of us. Summer houses are opened, grills are dusted off, the picnic table is repainted, and we get ready to start enjoying the outdoors in earnest.

A lot of bad food is passed off simply because it was cooked outside on a grill. Grilling is certainly easy, but it is no guarantee by itself of good eating. The recipes and hints in this chapter won't let you down.

There is an almost limitless range of outdoor cooking devices, from the simplest charcoal grill to the most sophisticated gas cooker. Good food can be made on all of it. Keep in mind just a few points. The grill should be clean. Scrubbing with a wire brush will usually do the trick. Some people swear by spray-on oven cleaner (rinse with the hose). Grills are usually easier to clean soon after they are used rather than later. Just let them cool down enough to handle.

Another point: *read the instructions* that come with your grill. The more complicated it is, the more you need to pay attention to what the manufacturer has worked hard to prepare for you.

Of course, you want to observe normal safety precautions. The grill and the utensils used on it get very hot and take a long time to cool down. Provide a safe place to put them to cool, especially electric charcoal starters. They are good and efficient at getting the coals going, but they have to be handled with respect for their very high temperature at the time they are removed from the coals.

Do-Ahead Barbecue Picnic

As for all holiday cooking, do as much as you can ahead. Remember to order major food items well in advance—spareribs and butterflied legs of lamb go like hotcakes as the big picnic-cookout weekend approaches. Decide on the guest list and get the invitations out early.

From your supply of dishes choose the ones you wouldn't mind terribly getting chipped, and use napkins you can live with if they get a little stained. Or use disposable things. The point is to be carefree and have a good time—hard to do if you are worried about the plates.

If guests volunteer to bring something, by all means let them. If they ask what they might bring, have your list ready and tell them what would best fit into your scheme. Perhaps someone will volunteer to pick up the ice at the last minute. Someone else might bring soft drinks or beer. Fine. Perhaps someone makes divine French bread. Cultivate these helpful souls. Contributed desserts could make your life easier. We'll concentrate here on some very good and slightly unusual grilled foods and a couple of variations on standard picnic dishes.

Do-Ahead Barbecue Picnic (for 8 or more)

Country Spareribs
Grilled Butterflied Leg of Lamb
Chicken Dinner In-a-Bag
Herbed Grilled Fish
Chinese Cabbage Coleslaw
New Potato Salad
Real Strawberry Shortcake

You wouldn't want to make all of this food for eight to twelve people. Choose on the basis of your guests' tastes and the number of mouths you have to feed.

Country Spareribs

1 whole rack of pork ribs, 5 to 6 pounds
1 medium-size onion, finely chopped
4 celery stalks, finely chopped
1 teaspoon ground cinnamon
2 cups catsup
1 tablespoon red wine vinegar
 Freshly ground black pepper

Up to several days before the cookout, put the rack of ribs in a very large, heavy pot and barely cover with water. Bring to a boil, then reduce heat so water simmers. Simmer 30 to 45 minutes, until the meat is almost, but not quite, done.

Remove ribs to drain; discard cooking water.

Make all-purpose barbecue sauce by mixing the remaining ingredients. Marinate ribs in the sauce in the refrigerator until ready to grill.

Remove ribs from marinade and grill until very tender and nicely browned, basting with marinade several times; 20 to 30 minutes should do it.

Hint: This method of precooking ribs gets rid of a lot of fat. It also speeds up the final grilling and lets you get a jump on preparation.

Grilled Butterflied Leg of Lamb

1 leg of lamb (4 to 5 lbs.)
½ cup olive oil
¼ cup lemon juice
4 or 5 garlic cloves
1 medium-size onion, sliced thin
2 teaspoons dried thyme
2 bay leaves
 Salt and pepper

Have your butcher bone and butterfly a leg of lamb. Place meat in a shallow baking dish and pour oil and lemon juice over it. Squeeze garlic in a press and spread evenly over meat. Add onion slices, thyme, and bay leaves. Sprinkle with salt and freshly ground pepper to taste.

Marinate the meat for 4 hours or more in the refrigerator, turning it at least once.

When you're ready to grill, remove lamb from marinade and place on grill over direct heat. Grill 4 to 5 minutes on each side.

To serve, slice thin across the grain, as you would London broil. The meat should be well browned on the outside, pink inside.

Hints: Do not be alarmed if the oil from the marinade and the fat from the lamb cause the coals to flame up when you put the meat on the grill. The flames will help sear the outside of the meat.

If you have a good supply of fresh mint, by all means chop up some of the leaves and add them to the marinade.

Chicken Dinner In-a-Bag

This very easy all-in-one meal is especially convenient on a gas grill, but charcoal also works.

2 **frying chickens (approx. 3 lbs. each), cut into serving pieces (or 6 lbs. chicken parts)**
8 **carrots, halved lengthwise**
1 **large or 2 medium-size onions, roughly chopped**
4 **celery stalks, sliced**
8 **new potatoes, scrubbed but not peeled**
2 **garlic cloves, peeled**
2 **bay leaves**
1 **teaspoon thyme**
1 **teaspoon rosemary**
1 **teaspoon tarragon**
¾ **cup dry white wine**
  Salt and pepper

Make a double-layer foil packet large enough to hold all the ingredients, with ends long enough to form a seal. On it arrange chicken pieces. Place vegetables and spices over and around the chicken. Pour on wine and season with salt and pepper to taste.

Seal packet tightly and place on a gas grill over medium heat for 15 minutes. Then close the grill cover, reduce heat as much as possible, and cook for 45 minutes more. If you are using a charcoal grill, move packet to one side after 15 minutes. Check chicken for doneness after 30 minutes cooking time.

To serve, slit foil and serve directly from the packet. Make sure everybody gets some of everything.

Hint: French or Italian bread is very good to sop up the juices.

Herb Grilled Fish

A double-sided wire broiler that is hinged to open and can be fastened firmly together to hold food makes broiling fish and other delicate foods easy on a grill.

2 whole white-fleshed fish (3 to 4 lbs.)
   Butter or margarine, softened
1 tablespoon minced fresh sage
1 tablespoon fresh rosemary
1 or 2 tablespoons fresh basil leaves
   Juice of 1 lemon
   Freshly ground black pepper
   Lemon slices or wedges

Wipe whole cleaned fish inside and out with paper towels. Rub both inside and outside generously with softened butter or margarine. Place herbs inside fish with lemon juice and pepper.

Arrange fish on a double-sided wire broiling rack and lock in place, or lay fish on a single sheet of heavy-duty foil over medium heat on the grill. Do not cover. Grill 5 minutes on each side and check for doneness. If the flesh is opaque and fairly firm to the touch, the fish is done; do not overcook. If more cooking is needed, grill another 2 or 3 minutes on each side.

Serve at once with plenty of lemon.

Hints: Have the fishmonger take the backbone out of the fish, but leave on the head and tail. This will make the fish much easier to serve and eat.

If you have been casting about for some new dishes to make for a picnic, you may want to try recipes that follow. These are adult foods rather than kiddie foods.

Chinese Cabbage Coleslaw

6 cups shredded Chinese cabbage
2 green bell peppers, chopped
1 red bell pepper, chopped
1 cup chopped celery
1 cup well-drained crushed pineapple (optional)
Slightly Different Dressing

Combine all ingredients except the dressing. Toss coleslaw with dressing 20 minutes before the meal is served so cabbage can marinate.

Slightly Different Dressing

4 garlic cloves, peeled
1 teaspoon salt
½ cup rice wine vinegar or white vinegar
1 tablespoon soy sauce
1 cup vegetable (not olive) oil

Press garlic through a garlic press. In a small bowl stir the garlic with the salt. Add the vinegar and soy sauce.

Add the oil in a steady stream while beating hard with a whisk. Beat thoroughly before tossing with cabbage.

Another good and unusual coleslaw is one of the simplest:

Red Balloon Coleslaw

1 large head cabbage, shredded
1 small can crushed pineapple, thoroughly drained
1 cup (8 oz.) sour cream
 Caraway seeds

Mix everything together just before serving. That's it!

New Potato Salad

The first tiny potatoes of the new season should be available about now. This slightly sophisticated potato salad uses them as a base.

24 small new potatoes, washed but not peeled
 1 medium-size onion, finely chopped, or 4 scallions, green
  part and all, sliced into ⅛-inch pieces
 3 celery stalks, finely chopped
 4 parsley sprigs, chopped
 4 fresh dill sprigs, chopped
¼ cup good white wine vinegar with tarragon
 1 cup olive oil
 Salt and freshly ground pepper

Cook the potatoes until they are just tender. Let cool enough to handle.

While potatoes cook and cool, prepare the other vegetables and mix vinegar and oil for the dressing.

Cut larger potatoes into 2 or 3 pieces; leave the very small ones whole. In a large bowl toss potatoes with all other ingredients. If you need more dressing, make it on the same 1-to-4 basis.

Hint: Add a small amount of mayonnaise to the potato salad if it seems very dry or if your guests rebel.

The strawberry season should be at its height. What better way to close the festivities than with genuine strawberry shortcake?

Real Strawberry Shortcake

Many people have never tasted real shortcake made with biscuits. Once you have, you will not want to go back to sponge cake cups, or indeed anything oversweet, as a bed for the berries.

 3 pints strawberries, washed, hulled, and sliced
¼ to ½ cup sugar
  Biscuits
  Whipped cream, slightly sweetened

Mix the berries and sugar and let stand at least 1 hour at room temperature.

Make biscuits.

Place bottoms of buttered biscuits on serving plates. Ladle sweetened strawberries over. Cover with top half of buttered biscuits and add more berries. Top with whipped cream.

Biscuits

 2 cups flour
 3 teaspoons baking powder
 1 teaspoons salt
½ cup solid vegetable shortening
1½ cups milk (approx.)
 Butter

Heat oven to 475°F.

Mix dry ingredients well. Work shortening into flour mixture until it resembles coarse meal; your hands are really the best tools for this job.

Add milk cautiously and stir with a wooden spoon (the hands are really messy here) to form a soft dough. Because flour differs, you may not need all the milk or you may need a little more.

Turn dough out onto a floured board and with floured hands knead the dough 4 or 5 times. Pat out into a flattened circle.

Roll dough to about ¾ inch thick. Cut individual biscuits 2½ to 3 inches in diameter.

Bake on an ungreased cookie sheet until golden brown, about 10 minutes. Check often so they do not overbrown.

When biscuits are done, split each one and generously butter.

Hints: If you wish to make a large single cake instead of individual biscuits, pat the dough into 2 circles, each about 8 inches in diameter and ¾ thick. (If you have dough left over, bake it into smaller biscuits.) Split each cake in half and build one large 4-layer shortcake.

The shortcake will improve by being assembled up to a few hours before it is served, but add the whipped cream at the last minute. This dessert should stand at room temperature, not in the refrigerator.

The biscuit base works fine on all sorts of fruit shortcakes. Use it with sliced peaches, blueberries, raspberries (especially good). You can use frozen fruits out of season.

7

☆ ☆ ☆ ☆ ☆ ☆ ☆ ☆ ☆ ☆

The Fourth of July

THREE CHEERS FOR THE RED, WHITE, AND BLUE! THIS MOST American of holidays reminds us that we have a lot to cheer for. It also provides a welcome holiday break in the middle of the summer. Many families find it is a good time for a family reunion: there is time to travel if necessary and reliably pleasant weather for outdoor activities.

By their very nature, these parties usually involve a *lot* of people. If you are daunted by the prospect of feeding up to twenty-five guests without killing yourself or going broke, take heart. You can do it with a combination of careful planning, cooking ahead, and delegating tasks.

As with other party menus, it is usually easier to make several dishes in their normal amounts than to try to make tons of a few things—who has pans that big? And don't forget the obvious: you'll have hamburgers and hot dogs on the grill, and you'll lay in a supply of potato and taco chips. Put a tub with ice and soft drinks in a shady spot and let people help themselves. On this occasion, people can drink from the cans or bottles; don't even think of trying to provide glasses (all that washing up) or cups (all that picking up). Use disposable plates and paper napkins.

All-American Picnic

Be sure to get an early start on preparations.

1. Up to two weeks before July 4:
   Shop for nonperishables and paper products. The pretty red, white, and blue stuff gets away early.

89

Line up your ice supply. Start stockpiling ice in your freezer if you have room; otherwise find out who will have ice when you need it.

2. One week before July 4:

Check out the place where your picnic will be held. If it is your backyard, does it need some grooming? Are there enough places to sit? You don't have to provide seating for all the people at the same time, but you need some—for older people and for disabled guests, for instance. Decide where you will put the food.

3. July 2:

Shop for the rest of the food. Things like hamburger buns have a way of disappearing from store shelves any later.

Make gazpacho, cover tightly, and store it in the refrigerator.

Make vinaigrette for the cold vegetables.

Make or buy the cakes for the Old Glory Cake. When they are completely cool, wrap tightly and store at room temperature.

Start thawing the frozen whipped topping to frost cake.

4. July 3:

Rest up.

Line up your cleanup crew: someone to collect the debris, someone to clean the grill, someone to supervise dishwashing.

5. July 4:

A few hours before your picnic is to begin, spray the picnic area well with insect repellent. Spray the grass and the shrubs. By party time the smell will have gone, but so will a good many of the bugs. Enjoy!

All-American Picnic (for 25)

Gazpacho   Marinated Vegetables Vinaigrette
Genuine Fried Chicken
Much Easier Fake Fried Chicken
Simply Splendid Deviled Eggs   Five Bean Salad
Baked Beans   Grilled Corn on the Cob
Hamburgers and Hot Dogs As Usual   Biscuits
Mexican Corn Bread   Old Glory Cake

Gazpacho

- **2 garlic cloves**
- **6 pounds tomatoes, trimmed**
- **1 large green pepper**
- **4 cucumbers**
- **1 large onion**
- **1 quart tomato juice**
- **⅔ cup olive oil**
- **¼ cup red wine vinegar**
- **Hot pepper sauce**
- **Salt and freshly ground pepper**

Peel the garlic and tomatoes, seed the green pepper, and roughly cut up the cucumbers and onion. Combine the vegetables, tomato juice, oil, and vinegar and process them in batches in a blender until roughly chopped; don't worry about proportions in each batch. Mix the processed vegetables all together in a large bowl, stir, and store in a *big* pitcher or jar with a tight lid in the refrigerator until serving time.

Taste soup and add salt, pepper, and hot sauce when it is thoroughly chilled.

To serve, give soup a stir or shake. The easiest was to serve it is in a pitcher, but if you have a soup tureen with a ladle, use it. Chill the tureen, fill it with soup, and set it out.

Hints: If you serve this soup in disposable mugs instead of bowls, you won't need to provide spoons.

If tomatoes are not at their best yet, consider using cherry tomatoes or Italian plum tomatoes. Either of these usually has more taste early in the season than other varieties.

If you like parsley especially, a handful in the soup would be good. Cilantro will also give the gazpacho a fresh taste. Just process it along with the other ingredients, or chop it up and use to garnish chilled soup.

Marinated Vegetables Vinaigrette

⅔ **cup olive oil**
⅓ **cup good red wine vinegar**
3 **tablespoons chopped pimiento-stuffed olives**
¼ **cup chopped scallions, green part and all**
¼ **cup chopped parsley**
   **Assorted vegetables such as raw carrot sticks, celery
   sticks, broccoli florets, cauliflower florets, cooked cold
   broccoli spears, steamed chilled green beans, steamed
   or canned asparagus, artichoke hearts**

Mix oil and vinegar and let the vinaigrette stand at least 1
hour at room temperature, stirring occasionally. Then store
tightly covered in the refrigerator until serving time.
   Arrange vegetables on a platter and drizzle vinaigrette over
them.

Genuine Fried Chicken

A lot of nonsense has been written about fried chicken. The
cooking method is easy: just keep heat moderate and don't
turn the chicken to death. This recipe is the real thing. There's
no getting around the fact that it is some work, but worth it.

4 **frying chickens (approx. 3 lb. each)**
   Flour
   Paprika
   Salt and pepper
   Vegetable oil
   Butter
   Bacon fat

Cut the chickens into pieces. You should get eight pieces
out of each: two wings (tuck tip under long bone to make
triangle), two breast pieces, two thighs, and two drumsticks.
(Freeze bony chicken backs and giblets for soup in cooler

weather.) Rinse chicken pieces and pat dry with paper towels.

Set out flour canister, paprika, salt and pepper, and the cooking fats. Mix 1 cup flour and 1 teaspoon each of paprika, salt, and pepper in a paper or plastic bag. You will need to do this three or four times, but this is a manageable quantity to work with.

In your largest heavy skillet or in an electric skillet heat the oil over medium heat (375°F. for electric skillet), and then add the butter and bacon fat. You will need about ½ inch of shortening in all. Start with 1 cup oil, ¼ cup butter, and 1 tablespoon bacon fat.

Dredge chicken pieces in seasoned flour. Shake off excess flour and arrange chicken pieces, skin side down, in the hot fat. Cook a few pieces at a time and do not crowd the skillet. Start thighs, drumsticks, and wings first, since they will take 35 to 40 minutes. Fry breast pieces about 25 minutes in all. Check on how chicken is browning when half the cooking time has passed. When the pieces are golden brown and crusty, turn them skin side up and continue cooking until the other side is browned and chicken is fork-tender. You need to turn only once. Add more shortening between batches as necessary. Keep heat moderate.

Drain fried chicken on paper towels or brown paper. You can keep it hot for an hour or so in a very slow (250°F.) oven, but it also tastes good at room temperature.

Hints: You can buy a similar number of chicken pieces instead of using whole chickens. Get the pieces your family likes best.

If you are lucky enough to have access to home-grown or other free-range chickens, you may find that they need a little more cooking time than battery-raised chicken that are available in supermarkets. If free-range chicken pieces are not completely tender before they are browned, add a tablespoon of water to the skillet, partially cover, and let steam for a few minutes. Then remove lid so that crust can crisp up again.

Chicken spits as it fries, so you are likely to have quite a mess on top of the stove. Be prepared to give it a good cleaning after the holiday. Always keeping the heat moderate helps control the splattering. Some.

Much Easier Fake Fried Chicken

If you still quail at the thought of making genuine fried chicken for twenty-five people, there is another solution. This type of chicken is not quite as good but very nearly. Unless you tell them, people may never know.

**4 frying chickens (approx. 3 lb.each), cut into
serving pieces
Milk to cover chicken
1 bag (4 to 6 oz.) potato chips**

Rinse the chicken and pat it dry with paper towels. Place it in a large bowl and cover with milk. Tightly cover and let stand in the refrigerator at least 4 hours or overnight.

Heat the oven to 350°F.

Take chicken out of milk and shake off excess liquid but do not pat dry. Crush potato chips fairly fine in their unopened bag, then slit the bag carefully lengthwise and open out to make a shallow bowl. Roll chicken pieces in crushed chips and arrange in a single layer, skin side up, in a shallow ungreased baking pan. Discard the milk used to marinate the chicken.

Bake for about 45 minutes, until chicken is fork-tender. If necessary, drain on paper towels before serving hot or at room temperature.

Simply Splendid Deviled Eggs

Deviled eggs seem like such a good idea, but often they are disappointing. These are not.

**2 dozen hard-boiled eggs, shelled
½ cup mayonnaise
3 tablespoons dry sherry
1 tablespoon white wine vinegar or lemon juice
3 tablespoons slightly browned melted butter
2 teaspoons grated onion
Salt and freshly ground pepper
1 teaspoon dry mustard (optional)
Assorted garnishes such as tiny shrimps, shrimp salad,
rolled anchovies, olives, parsely, caviar, and capers.**

Carefully cut the eggs in half lengthwise. Scoop yolks into a bowl or put them into the container of a food processor fitted with the plastic blade. Add all other ingredients except the garnishes. Mix with a fork or process until smooth. Use a little more vinegar or mayonnaise if mixture is very crumbly.

Stuff egg whites with a spoon or by piping the yolk mixture into them with the medium-sized star tip from a cake decorating set.

Garnish eggs with tiny canned shrimp or salad shrimp from the fish market, rolled anchovies, green or black olive halves, parsley sprigs, tiny bits of red or black caviar, or a caper or two. You have 48 pieces to work with, so let your imagination run.

Arrange eggs on a serving plate and chill until serving time.

Hint: It would be nice to tell you to cook the eggs for these deviled eggs ahead of time, but they really do taste better if you boil them the morning you plan to use them, let them cool, then peel them and deal with them right away. They also taste better if they get thoroughly chilled before serving.

Five Bean Salad

This is the old favorite but with a twist: it is served hot!

1 pound bacon
5 or 6 large onions, fairly finely chopped
1 cup cider vinegar
4 tablespoons prepared mustard
1 cup brown sugar
2 cans (16 oz. each) baby lima eans, drained
2 cans (16 oz. each) red or pink kidney beans with juice
2 cans (16 oz. each) garbanzo beans, drained
2 cans (16 oz. each) navy or pinto beans, drained
2 cans (16 oz. each) green or wax beans, drained
2 cloves garlic, finely chopped
Salt and freshly ground pepper

Fry bacon until very crisp, but don't scorch it. When it is done, remove from skillet, drain on paper towels, wrap, and refrigerate.

Sauté onion in bacon fat. When it is translucent but not browned, add vinegar, mustard, and brown sugar. Let the mixture simmer 2 or 3 minutes.

Combine all of the beans in an ovenproof casserole. Pour onion mixture over beans and mix well. Add garlic and salt and pepper to taste.

You can assemble this dish a day or two ahead. Store, tightly covered, in the refrigerator.

An hour or two before serving, heat oven to 350°F. Crumble reserved bacon and sprinkle over bean casserole. Heat for 1 to 1½ hours. Serve hot or at room temperature.

Baked Beans

Many people don't feel they've been to a picnic if they don't have baked beans. If you want to make them from scratch, you will find the results very rewarding.

2 pounds navy beans
2 teaspoons salt, or to taste
½ cup brown sugar
1 tablespoon dry mustard
½ cup molasses
1 medium-size onion, chopped fairly fine
½ pound salt pork, sliced

Look over beans and rinse in cold water. Cover with water by at least 2 inches and let soak overnight.

Drain beans. Put in a large cooking pot with a lid, cover with fresh water by at least 2 inches. Add salt. Bring to a boil, then reduce heat so that it water remains at a lively simmer. Partially cover and cook for about 1 hour.

Drain the beans, reserving the cooking liquid.

In a large heavy ovenproof casserole combine the beans with everything else but the salt pork. Add 3½ cups of the reserved cooking liquid. Add water if necessary to make up amount. Arrange sliced salt pork on top of beans. Cover.

Bake in a 300°F. oven for 5 to 7 hours, or overnight in a 275°F. oven. Check occasionally. Add more water if necessary. Beans should not dry out until they are very tender and the salt pork is tender. Uncover the casserole for the last hour or so of baking to let beans brown and pork crisp.

Serve hot or warm.

Hints: Obviously this is not a dish that can be made at the last minute, but you can make it ahead and store in the refrigerator. It is even better reheated. Just make sure there is enough liquid.

These baked beans will not look like baked beans until near the end of the baking process. Don't panic.

Grilled Corn on the Cob

It is unlikely that there will be local corn on the cob by July, but if you can find some, an excellent way to prepare it is on the grill. Alternatively, you can always put a big pot of water on the kitchen stove.

Corn, still in the husks, (as much as your crowd can eat)
Butter
Salt and pepper

Loosen but do not remove husks. Remove and discard most of the cornsilk. Carefully replace husks around corn cobs.

Soak corn in husks in a large tub or sink full of cold water for 20 minutes.

Arrange corn in a single layer on a hot grill and cook for about 15 minutes. Turn frequently with long tongs.

Remove corn from grill and serve with butter and salt and pepper.

Hints: The best way to get the husks off the grilled corn is to grasp the cornsilk end with a heavy oven mitt and chop ½ to 1 inch off the stem end. The husks will fall away. A cleaver or heavy knife will do it.

If your corn should get husked while you're not looking, wrap each ear in a double layer of heavy-duty foil and grill as directed.

Biscuits

Make biscuits (page 86). If you need more, make another batch. Do not butter biscuits; let your guests butter or not as they see fit.

Mexican Corn Bread

2 recipes corn bread batter (page 34)
8 ounces Monterey Jack cheese
½ cup canned jalapeño peppers packed in *water*, drained and chopped

Make corn bread batter. Heat oven to 450°F. and melt shortening in two 8 × 8-inch baking pans or 8-inch cast-iron skillets.

Grate cheese and divide it between the 2 batches of dough. Add half the jalapeños to each batch; mix well.

Pour each batch of batter into a hot greased pan or skillet and bake 20 to 25 minutes, until nicely browned. Transfer to serving plates and serve hot.

Hints: If your family really loves cheese and hot peppers, use more to taste. The quantities given here will make a lively bread but not a red-hot one.

This corn bread really tastes best when it's hot. If it needs reheating, do so gently in a 200°F. oven or heat for 1 to 1½ minutes in a microwave.

Old Glory Cake

This cake takes a little doing, but it is more impressive looking than it is difficult to make.

You can buy the yellow or white cakes. If you want to bake them, consider using two packages cake mix made according to package instructions. Bake each cake in a 9 × 13-inch baking dish or pan. When cool, trim ends to produce 9 × 12-inch rectangles.

2 pints strawberries
1 cup red currant jelly
1 pint blueberries
2 thick rectangular white or yellow cakes (9 × 12 in. each)
Strawberry jam
2 large packages frozen whipped topping, thawed

Wash, drain well, and carefully slice the strawberries lengthwise. Use berries as near the same size as possible to make uniform slices.

Melt currant jelly over simmering water in a double boiler or heat 1 or 2 minutes in microwave. Let cool. Add 1 teaspoon water if it begins to jell again.

Dip each slice of strawberry into the currant jelly. Lay in a single layer on foil to drain and dry out a little.

Wash, look over, and very thoroughly drain the blueberries. Let them dry completely on paper towels.

Spread one cake with strawberry jam and stack the second cake above it to form a top layer. Frost top and sides of the two-layer with thawed cake whipped topping.

Using your kitchen ruler measure the field of blue in the upper left-hand corner of the cake. It will be a rectangle 4½ inches high by 6¾ inches wide along the 12-inch dimension of the cake. Very carefully fill entire rectangle with a single layer of blueberries. Cover as much of the area as possible with berries.

Make a red stripe with the jelly-coated strawberry slices along the top and bottom edges of the cake. Make another stripe below and touching the bottom of the field of blue. Now make two rows of strawberry slices between the top and middle stripes and two more between the middle and bottom stripes. Fill in the white stripes with more whipped topping using a ¾-inch plain tip from a cake decorating set.

In a 3¾-inch circle in the field of blue, make thirteen stars with the medium star tip of a cake decorating set. The top two are where the minute hand would be at 10:52 and 12:03 on a clock. Space the other eleven evenly around the circle.

Refrigerate the cake until serving time.

Hints: You really need to assemble the cake the morning it is to be used.

Putting the white stripes on last gives you a chance to clean up any little mistakes from the strawberries.

The best way to handle the strawberry slices and blueberries is with long kitchen tweezers. Be gentle.

Don't even think of trying to put fifty stars in the field of blue. I know somebody who tried it. Once. Thirteen stars in a circle were good enough for Betsy Ross.

A Real Nice Clambake Miles from the Shore (for 8)

Even if you live far inland, you can have a clambake to celebrate July Fourth or any other special occasion. Just locate your sources early to make sure you get the shellfish you need. It is possible to order already-assembled clambakes in their own pot. Very nice, but very expensive. You pay for the service.

The number of people you can feed at an inland done-on-the-grill clambake will really depend on how big your really big pot is. It has to hold the whole meal for however many people you plan on having. If you're willing to build a fire and blacken a washtub, you can invite more people.

There are several advantages to cooking even a landlocked clambake outdoors, the first of which is that it keeps all that heat out of the kitchen in a season when that may be very desirable. It will also be less messy to clean up after serving and eating outdoors. And you will have enough room to move around.

Increase or decrease amounts to suit your party. To give an idea of the proportions, here is a top-of-the-grill clambake for eight.

Landlocked Clambake

  8 large baking potatoes, scrubbed but not peeled
 16 ears of corn in husks
  8 chicken pieces (optional)
 16 hard-shell clams or soft-shell steamers
  8 lobsters (approx. 1½ lb. each)
  1 quart (approx.) clam broth
  2 pounds butter

Thoroughly scrub and rinse the big pot or tub you plan to use. Put it on the grill over high heat with about 2 inches of water in the bottom. Start cooking the potatoes about 45 minutes before you plan to eat.

Carefully pull husks of corn back and remove as much corn-silk as possible. Replace husks. Set corn aside.

If you are using chicken, add it to the steamer 30 minutes before you plan to eat. Add more boiling water if necessary. Cover pot.

Twenty minutes before you want to eat, stand the corn ears around the edge of the pot, or remove chicken, put the corn directly above the potatoes, and place the chicken on top of the corn. If you are using soft-shell clams, add them now. Cover pot.

Fifteen minutes before you plan to eat, put well rinsed lobsters into the pot and cover tightly. If you are using hard-shelled clams add them five minutes later. Open the bottles of clam broth and place them in the pot to warm up. Cut the butter into small pieces, place it in a jar, and set it in the pot to melt. As soon as the clams open (discard any that do not), you are ready to feast. Serve the clam juice and butter in individual dishes for dipping.

Hints: If the potatoes need a little more cooking, cover the pot and let them cook a few more minutes. Meanwhile, get on with the clams and lobster while they are hot.

The easiest way to melt and serve the butter is in wide-mouthed small jars, like the ones marinated artichoke hearts come in. Divide the butter, cut it in chunks, put each portion in a jar, put the lid on, and place jars in pot with clams. Fish out jars with a heavy oven mitt at serving time.

If you feel something else is needed, you might offer a green salad with a simple oil and vinegar dressing and French or Italian bread to sop up juices. If anyone can face dessert, let that person go and buy it and bring it back.

If you like the idea of a clambake but don't want to go to quite so much trouble, you might serve Mussels à la Marinière. You need to like mussels, be able to get a good supply of them, and have a big pot to cook them in.

Mussels à la Marinière

1 pound mussels in their shells for each person to be
   served
½ cup chopped fresh parsley
3 scallions, green part and all, chopped
2 garlic cloves, roughly chopped
   Enough good dry white wine to cover the bottom of
   the pot ¼- to ½-inch deep (approx. 2 cups)
   French or Italian bread

Wash the mussels under cold running water. Let them stand
in a big pot under dripping cold water for at least 1 hour
(longer wouldn't hurt). Before cooking, scrub each mussel
with a nail brush and discard any that are open. Trim off the
beards with nail scissors.

About 20 minutes before you plan to eat, put all ingredients
into a big pot. Place over high heat. Check in 10 minutes.
When the mussels open, you are ready to eat. Serve each person a portion of mussels and broth in a large soup bowl. Provide French or Italian bread to sop up broth (essential).

Hints: If your guests really love mussels, double this recipe.
Serve the rest of the dry white wine with the mussels.

If you serve only a moderate number of mussels, you might
be able to face a green salad and a light dessert. You can make
one of this pie or as many as you need early in the day they
are to be served.

Lemon Meringue Pie

For every six people you will need one pie.

1 piecrust recipe (page 115) or prepared dough from
   supermarket refrigerator case
1 cup sugar
3 tablespoons cornstarch
   Dash salt
2 egg yolks

3 tablespoons cold water
1 lemon
1 cup very hot water
1 tablespoon butter

Bake piecrust and let it cool completely.

Put sugar, cornstarch, salt, egg yolks, and cold water in a heavy saucepan and mix to make a smooth paste.

Grate rind of lemon into sugar mixture. Squeeze the lemon and strain the juice. Add it gradually to the saucepan, stirring.

Add hot water and butter. Cook over medium heat, stirring constantly, until mixture boils.

Pour lemon mixture into the piecrust. Let cool completely.

Meringue

2 egg whites at room temperature
Dash salt
¼ teaspoon cream of tartar
4 tablespoons confectioners' sugar

Beat egg whites, salt, and cream of tartar until stiff but still glossy.

Add sugar, 1 tablespoon at a time, and continue beating until all sugar is dissolved.

Pile meringue on cooled pie filling and spread out with spatula. Be sure to seal meringue to edges of piecrust. Brown 15 to 20 minutes in an oven that has been preheated to 400°F. *then turned off.*

Hints: The best utensil for sealing the meringue to the crust so that it won't shrink as it browns is a narrow rubber spatula, the kind used with the blender or food processor.

Lemon Meringue Pie is at its very best served just after it cools from having the meringue browned. Store leftovers in the refrigerator, of course, though it won't do the meringue any good.

There you have it: big celebrations, medium-size parties, positively intimate get-togethers. Have a great Fourth!

8

(((((((((

Halloween

THE WEEKS BEFORE HALLOWEEN ARE GOING TO BE THE LAST relatively peaceful time before the major holiday festivities. Yes, peaceful. Getting costumes together and finding the perfect pumpkins for jack-o'-lanterns are daily tasks, but trust me, this time is peaceful compared to the next two months. Use it to get a jump on the year-end holidays. Cooking and baking now may seem like rushing the season, but when it arrives you'll be glad to be prepared. Now the count down!

1. Any time after Labor Day, mix up Cheese-Sausage Balls (see page 114) and freeze them, and bake them as needed for the coming holiday parties.
2. One week before Halloween:
    Get your knives sharpened. Do it yourself, or if they have passed that point, appeal to your butcher. Some butchers will sharpen knives, or at least refer you to the people who sharpen their knife blades. Remember especially the knife in the carving set. It will be seeing a lot of duty between now and the New Year.
    Check baking equipment. It is tedious to do serious baking without the proper utensils. A minimum list includes the following:

    3 cookie sheets in good condition
    4 two-inch 12-muffin tins (sometimes called "tea gems") and paper liners Most regular recipes will fill 4 of these pans. Remember all the times you've been asked to produce a hundred of something for a bake sale or school function? Twice around in these will do 96. Bake by standing two pans on each cookie sheet.

105

 2 three-inch 12-muffin tins and paper liners
 1 ten-inch tube pan and/or one 10-inch bundt pan loaf
    pans to suit your family's size, say 2 large (9 × 5
    inches), 2 medium (7 × 3 inches)
 2 large 9 × 13-inch ovenproof glass baking dishes
 2 medium 7 × 11-inch ovenproof glass baking dishes
    an assortment of heatproof and ovenproof casseroles
    with lids
12 three-inch ovenproof glass custard cups

If your refrigerator uses ice trays, look at the ones you
have. Leaks? Get new ones. They are inexpensive,
and the last thing you need now is ice pyramids in
your freezer. Check your supply of wooden spoons
and spatulas and rubber and plastic spatulas. These
items wear out; now is a good time to restock.

Stock up on aluminum foil, plastic storage bags, plastic
wrap, and waxed paper.

Check potholders. It is tedious and *dangerous* to do a
lot of serious cooking without potholders in good
condition. Get what you need. Think of it as acci-
dent insurance.

Check all of your kitchen linens. Your kitchen will get
a lot of visitors soon. Do you have dish towels wor-
thy of public appearance? Do your effective potholders look good enough to display?

Check your candle supply and replenish as necessary.
Did you ever try to buy red and green candles the
week before Christmas? Make sure you know how
the candles smell when lit. You don't want any per-
fumy scents or heavy petroleum smells around food.

Polish your silver. Try dip-type liquid; it does a very
good job on seriously tarnished flat silver and serving pieces such as coffee services and trays. Follow
package directions. Store flatware in plastic bags;
squeeze out all the air you can and close snugly with
a twist tie. The silver will stay pristine and will not
develop the off taste that it can get from nontarnish
cloth wraps and silver-chest linings. *Remember:* do
not put silver in the dishwasher with stainless steel.

Serious permanent etching can result. Hollow-handle knives seem especially vulnerable.

Shop for nonperishables for Halloween supper and the baking effort. Be sure to get a new package of baking powder; this is no time to take chances.

Cook everything ahead that you can and store it. You want to free up the kitchen and the pots and pans for the push to come.

3. Day before Halloween:

Shop for perishable groceries for supper and baking.

Seasonal Halloween Supper

> **Seasonable Halloween Supper** (for 12)
>
> Pumpkin-Mushroom Soup
> Vegetarian Chili   Vegetarian Ragout in a Pumpkin
> Black Cat Cookies
> Hot Chocolate with Jack-o'-Lantern Marshmallows

Pumpkin-Mushroom Soup

½ **pound mushrooms sliced ⅛ inch thick**
½ **chopped onion**
2 **tablespoons vegetable oil or butter**
2 **tablespoons flour**
1 **tablespoon curry powder**
1 **teaspoon cumin**
  Dash nutmeg
  Salt and pepper
  Hot pepper flakes
1 **tablespoon honey (optional)**
3 **cups chicken broth**
1 **can (16 oz.) pumpkin or 2 cups homemade pumpkin puree**
1 **cup light cream or unsweetened evaporated milk**
  Sour cream or yogurt

In a heavy soup pot sauté mushrooms and onion in oil. Add flour, spices, and salt, pepper, and hot pepper to taste. Cook over medium heat, stirring constantly, until flour is cooked but not browned, about 5 minutes.

Add honey, broth, and pumpkin and cook, stirring occasionally, over medium heat for 15 minutes. The soup can be made up to this point as much as three or four days ahead; cool and refrigerate, tightly covered.

Just before serving, add cream or milk and heat the soup through; do *not* allow it to boil. Serve in warmed bowls topped with a dollop of sour cream or yogurt.

Hints: This recipe will serve 12 as a first course. To serve it as a main dish, double everything. If you have any left over, it is very good served cold.

If you use homemade broth, you can stir in some slivers of leftover chicken.

Vegetarian Chili

This recipe has been polished to a high shine by a very good cook whose sister is mostly a vegetarian.

    1 can (14 oz.) crushed tomatoes
    2 cups water
    1 cup raw bulgur wheat
 1½ cups chopped onion
    4 garlic cloves, peeled and crushed
    1 cup sliced carrots
    1 cup chopped celery
    1 bay leaf
    2 teaspoons cumin
    3 dried chili peppers, crumbled, or 3 heaping
      tablespoons chili powder
  ½ teaspoon celery seed
  ½ teaspoon dried basil
  ½ teaspoon cayenne

1½ teaspoons salt
 1 cup chopped green bell pepper
 3 cans (16 oz. each) kidney beans, including liquid
   Assorted toppings such as shredded Monterey jack
   cheese, chopped onions, and hot pepper flakes.

In a large heavy pot with a tight-fitting lid bring crushed tomatoes and 1 cup of the water to a boil. Add bulgur wheat. Cover and turn off heat. Let stand for at least 15 minutes.

In a dry skillet over medium heat sauté onion and garlic until barely browned. Add carrots and celery. Stir so mixture does not burn. Cook 2 minutes, then add the remaining 1 cup water, all the spices, and the salt. Reduce heat to very low, cover the skillet, and simmer the sauce for 5 minutes.

Add the contents of the skillet to the tomato-wheat mixture in the big pot. Bring the mixture to a rolling boil, stirring often so bottom doesn't burn. Add green peppers and beans.

Lower heat so that the chili barely simmers. Cover and cook for at least 1 hour, stirring only once or twice.

Serve with toppings of grated Monterey jack cheese, fresh chopped onions, sour cream, hot pepper flakes, or whatever pleases your crowd.

Hints: Like many dishes of this kind, this one is better the day after it is cooked. Store tightly covered in the refrigerator; reheat at serving time.

If you cannot find bulgur wheat in the supermarket, try health food stores or Middle Eastern grocery stores. If you can't find it at all, serve the chili over brown rice (⅓ cup raw rice per person) cooked according to package directions.

You can make hotter or milder chili by varying the amounts of spices. The more you use, the longer the pot should simmer to amalgamate the flavors.

Vegetarian Ragout in a Pumpkin

This stew of savory vegetables and spices is most impressive in its tureen, a pumpkin.

1 pumpkin, 12 to 14 inches in diameter
2 large onions, roughly chopped
2 garlic cloves, peeled and roughly chopped
2 tablespoons margarine or vegetable oil
3 celery stalks, leaves and all, chopped
3 large carrots sliced in ½-inch diagonals
2 large parsnips sliced in ¼-inch diagonals
1 large unpeeled eggplant cut in 1-inch cubes
2 medium-size turnips cut in ¼-inch slices
4 unpeeled baking potatoes, scrubbed and cut in 1-inch cubes
6 cups vegetable stock or water
2 bay leaves
8 parsley sprigs, chopped
2 teaspoons dried rosemary
2 teaspoons dried thyme
3 or 4 peppercorns, crushed
Salt

Make an opening in the stem end of the pumpkin as for a jack-o'-lantern: cut a large circle with a small sharp knife, holding the point of the blade at an angle toward the center of the pumpkin. Remove top and clean out seeds and membranes. Replace top and set aside.

In a large heavy skillet, sauté onions and garlic in the margarine or oil until soft but not browned. Add celery and cook just until wilted.

Heat over to 350°F.

Put carrots, parsnips, eggplant, turnips, and potatoes in a large heavy pot. Add vegetable stock or water, spices, and salt to taste. Bring to a brisk boil. Add onions, garlic, and celery.

Place pumpkin on a cookie sheet with sides, remove top, and transfer boiling ragout to pumpkin. Cover the top of the pumpkin loosely with a piece of aluminum foil. Place in oven.

After 1 hour, reduce oven heat to 300°F. The ragout is done when the potatoes can be easily pierced with a fork, usually about 2 hours more. Be careful not to pierce the pumpkin shell.

About 1 hour before the ragout is done, remove foil and put the top of the pumpkin back in place.

To serve, put pumpkin, still on the cookie sheet, on the table on trivets or heatproof pads (it will be *very* hot). Scoop out some of the cooked pumpkin pulp with each serving. When the meal is finished, remove leftover ragout from pumpkin and store in another container in the refrigerator. Discard the pumpkin tureen; it has given its all.

Black Cat Cookies

These are basically sugar cookies done up for the season. It is hard to say how many each batch will make because sizes of cat-shaped cookie cutters vary. If you need more cookies, make another batch; this recipe is easier to handle in the quantities given.

2¼ **cups flour**
1 **teaspoon baking powder**
½ **cup sugar**
⅔ **cup vegetable shortening, margarine, or lard**
1 **egg**
1 **tablespoon water**
1 **teaspoon vanilla extract**
12 **ounces semisweet chocolate bits**

Heat oven to 425°F.

Sift flour, baking powder, and sugar together. Cut in shortening until the mixture looks like coarse meal.

Beat the egg slightly with water and vanilla extract and add all at once to the dry mixture. Use more water if necessary to make a very stiff dough. Stir and knead until dough is smooth.

Roll dough very thin on a floured board and cut out cat shapes. Place on ungreased cookie sheets and bake until light brown around the edges, 10 or 15 minutes. The cookies will not be crisp, so test by their color.

When the cookies are done, use a broad spatula to carefully transfer them to a rack to cool completely.

While cookies cool, melt chocolate bits in the top of a double boiler. When cookies are cool to the touch, place cooling rack over a large pan with sides and pour melted chocolate over the cookies to make a thin coating. Cool completely again, carefully remove from rack, and store in single layers separated by waxed paper, tightly covered, until ready to serve.

Hints: If you cannot find a cat-shaped cookie cutter, cut the dough in circles. Use a wooden toothpick or a small brush to draw a cat on each cookie with melted chocolate and carefully fill in the middle. Decorate with orange sprinkles.

If you have chocolate left over, save it. Just melt it again and pour it over cooled nut brittle. It is delicious.

If you have a microwave, melt the chocolate in it. Start with 1 minute. Stir. Chocolate melts without losing its shape in the microwave, so you must stir it to see how soft it really is.

Hot Chocolate with Jack-o'-Lantern Marshmallows

This hot chocolate is the real thing, what you probably remember from childhood.

For each serving:
2 tablespoons cocoa
1 tablespoon sugar
Dash salt
1 tablespoon hot water
¾ cup milk

In a large saucepan, blend cocoa, sugar, salt, and water. Cook over medium heat until smooth. Simmer 2 or 3 minutes to develop the flavor of the chocolate.

Add milk. Stir to mix thoroughly. Do not boil. Cover, remove from heat, and set aside until ready to serve.

To serve, reheat hot chocolate gently. Beat with a whisk to froth up slightly. Serve in warmed mugs with Jack-o'-Lantern Marshmallows.

Jack-o'-Lantern Marshmallows

1 package (8 to 10 oz.) marshmallows
Orange food coloring and green food coloring
Melted chocolate

Stand marshmallows on end on a sheet of foil or wax paper. With a wooden toothpick or a small brush draw a pumpkin on each marshmallow with orange food coloring. Paint a jack-o'-lantern face on the pumpkins with melted chocolate. Draw a green stem on top.
Let dry thoroughly.

Hints: If your food-coloring set does not have orange in it, shake a few drops of yellow coloring into a custard cup. Add red very slowly until orange is formed.

Don't worry about having too many marshmallows. They disappear in mysterious ways.

You can use this principle for other holiday marshmallows as well. For Christmas, draw two holly leaves, stem to stem, with green food coloring. Put a red-hot cinnamon candy between them as a holly berry. Very pretty. For Easter, draw a green nest of grass and add pastel miniature candies for Easter eggs or draw them. You could draw a yellow menorah for Chanukah. "Light" one more of the blue candles each night.

Serious Group Effort to Cook Ahead for the Year-End Holidays

Ask four or five like-minded friends to spend Halloween with you. Their kids can trick-or-treat, bob for apples (dry the apples off and serve them later with the cookies), and eat supper while the grown-ups cook and bake ahead and eat supper. Early in the day do the quicker-baking items, grouping those that need similar times and temperatures. Then tackle the fruit-cakes, which will bake for a long, long time. Steamed puddings (top of the stove) and candies can be made any time you can fit them in. Two ovens are helpful. Even better, two ovens and a cooperating next-door neighbor with two ovens! You are going to make several batches of each recipe and divide the booty. Invite your guests to bring baking pans for the projects they plan to take home. When you agree on projects to be done, shopping in bulk for the ingredients will probably save money. At least everything you need will be in place when you need it.

Check your oven's capacity. You can use both levels if you rotate the pans on the racks halfway through baking—remember those good potholders?

Cheese-Sausage Balls

1 pound sharp cheddar cheese, grated
1 pound hot bulk sausage or sausage links split, casings removed
3 cups dry biscuit mix

Let all ingredients come to room temperature.

Mix all ingredients together in a large bowl. Your hands are the best tool for the job.

Form dough into 1-inch balls. Freeze on a cookie sheet until very firm; shake frozen balls into double plastic bags and store in freezer.

Before serving, put as many balls as you will need on a cookie sheet and bake at 400°F. for 10 minutes. Balls will be light brown and very, very hot. Serve at once.

Hints: This recipe makes 180 (15 dozen) Cheese-Sausage Balls, but it is easier to work with these simple bulk amounts than to try to halve the recipe. These treats keep indefinitely in the freezer. You will be glad to have them on hand.

Cheese-Sausage Balls are very, very good as a snack with hot tea on a cold day.

Jam Cake

One year my mother did not get around to making fruitcakes for the holidays. She had a lot of homemade jam left from summers gone by, so she made a Jam Cake. She thought one would be enough, but we wound up eating several. The cake is pretty, festive, and delicious. And easy.

2 cups flour
3 teaspoons baking powder
1 teaspoon salt
2 cups sugar
½ teaspoon nutmeg
½ teaspoon ground cinnamon

¼ teaspoon ground cloves
1 cup raisins
1 cup nuts, roughly chopped
¾ cup vegetable oil
¾ cup orange juice or cider
3 eggs, lightly beaten
1 cup strawberry, blackberry, or raspberry jam

Heat oven to 300°F. Grease and flour a 10-inch tube or bundt pan.

Sift dry ingredients together into a large mixing bowl. Add raisins and nuts; stir to coat with flour.

Mix oil, juice, eggs, and jam. Blend into dry ingredients.

Turn batter into the prepared pan and bake for about 1 hour, until a cake tester comes out clean.

Cool cake 5 minutes in the pan, then turn out on a rack to cool completely. No frosting needed.

Store tightly wrapped in the freezer until two or three days before serving. Thaw and store at room temperature, covered.

Piecrust

1¼ cups flour
½ teaspoon salt
⅓ cup lard or vegetable shortening
3 or 4 tablespoons ice-cold water

Sift flour and salt together.

Work shortening into flour with fingers as quickly as possible.

Combine flour and shortening until mixture looks like very coarse meal. Add water one tablespoon at a time. As soon as all the flour is dampened and dough forms a ball, wrap it in wax paper or plastic and refrigerate for at least 30 minutes.

Roll out dough very thin on a floured board with a floured rolling pin or place it between sheets of wax paper and roll it out. Peel one piece of wax paper, invert crust over pie pan, and carefully peel off bottom paper. Do not stretch dough.

Trim dough ½ inch below edge of pie pan. Turn under extra dough and crimp or flute edges.

Prick bottom of piecrust several times with a fork.

If you are making crusts ahead, freeze in pans until very firm. Then you can store several stacked in 1 pan, each frozen crust wrapped in plastic film. If a pie calls for a baked piecrust, bake it in a pie pan in a 425°F. oven about 15 minutes, until golden brown just before using. No need to thaw before baking.

Hints: Lard makes the best and flakiest piecrusts.

If you have a food processor, fit bowl with steel blade, combine flour, salt, and shortening and pulse just until mixed. Add water a little at a time and process until a ball forms. Wrap, chill, and roll as directed above.

During this busy season you might consider using one of the very good prepared piecrusts available in supermarkets in the dairy case or the freezer. Follow package instructions.

Make two separate batches of piecrust dough rather than doubling this recipe.

Pecan Pie

⅓ **cup white sugar**
½ **cup brown sugar**
½ **cup light corn syrup**
¼ **cup butter or margarine**
4 **eggs, lightly beaten**
1 **teaspoon vanilla extract**
1½ **cups pecans broken into medium-size pieces**
1 **unbaked piecrust**

Heat oven to 300°F.

Combine sugars, syrup, and butter in a saucepan. Stir over medium heat until sugars and butter are melted.

Gradually add hot sugar-butter syrup to beaten eggs, stirring vigorously. Add vanilla extract.

Stir in pecans.

Pour filling into unbaked piecrust (do not overfill pan) and bake about 45 minutes, until the center of the pie is almost firm and starting to puff slightly.

Cool pie thoroughly on a rack. Put pie (pan and all) into a plastic bag, squeeze out all air, seal tightly, and freeze.

To serve, let pie thaw completely at room temperature. If you make the pie the day it is to be served, allow to cool completely before cutting (at least 2 hours).

Hints: This pie is very good made with English walnuts, too. The filling by itself with no nuts is Chess Pie. Very English and very good.

You are going to have to commit the pie pan to the pie since the frozen baked edge of the piecrust is too fragile for storage in just a plastic bag. You might want to use disposable foil pans.

Pound Cake

This is the real thing. It makes store-bought pound cakes taste store-bought. It freezes beautifully. It is *very important* to have all ingredients at room temperature before mixing batter.

¾ **pound butter**
3 **cups sugar**
5 **eggs**
3½ **cups flour**
½ **teaspoon baking powder**
¼ **teaspoon salt**
1 **cup milk**
1 **tablespoon vanilla extract**
1 **tablespoon lemon extract**

Heat over to 325°F.
Grease and flour a 10-inch tube or bundt pan.
Cream butter and sugar together. Add eggs one at a time and beat well.

Add dry ingredients alternately with milk (3 batches dry ingredients, 2 of milk). Mix thoroughly in between batches. Stir in flavorings.

Turn batter into prepared pan and bake 1½ hours or until a cake tester comes out clean and edges have drawn away from sides of pan slightly. Turn out on a rack to cool completely.

Freeze in airtight wrap. To serve, thaw and store covered at room temperature.

Cranberry Bread

3 cups flour
1 teaspoon baking powder
1 teaspoon baking soda
1 teaspoon salt
2 eggs lightly beaten
1 cup sugar
¼ cup melted butter or margarine, cooled
1¼ cups milk
1 cup raw cranberries, picked over before measuring
¾ cup chopped nuts

Heat oven to 350°F.
Grease and flour one 9 × 5-inch or two 7 × 3-inch loaf pans.
Sift dry ingredients together.
In a separate bowl mix eggs, sugar, melted butter, and milk.
Add to dry ingredients and mix only until dry ingredients are moistened thoroughly. Batter will be very thick. Gently fold in cranberries and nuts.
Turn batter into pans to fill two-thirds full. Bread will rise while baking, then settle somewhat.
Bake about 1 hour or until a cake tester comes out clean. Let stand in pan 5 minutes, then turn out on a rack to cool completely.
Wrap cooled loaves in airtight material and let stand at least overnight before serving. Or freeze for future use, thaw at room temperature, and store thawed loaves in the refrigerator.

Pumpkin Bread

2 cups pumpkin puree
3 cups sugar
⅔ cup water
⅔ cup vegetable oil
1 teaspoon ground cinnamon
½ teaspoon ground cloves
½ teaspoon salt
½ teaspoon baking powder
2 teaspoons baking soda

1 cup raisins
1 cup pecan pieces (optional)
3½ cups flour

Heat oven to 350°F.

Grease and flour three 7 × 3-inch loaf pans.

Beat together pumpkin, sugar, water, and oil. Add cinnamon, cloves, salt, baking powder, and soda. Mix well.

In a separate bowl mix raisins and nuts, if you wish, into flour and combine with pumpkin mixture, blending well.

Pour mixture into prepared pans and bake for 1 hour. A cake tester should come out clean, and bread should have begun to pull away from sides of pans.

Let bread cool completely on a rack. Freeze in airtight wrap. Thaw at room temperature and store in refrigerator. This bread is too delicate to go in the toaster, but it's very good toasted under the broiler.

Apricot Nut Bread

1¼ cups dried apricots
2½ cups flour
  3 teaspoons baking powder
  1 teaspoon salt
  ½ teaspoon baking soda
  ¼ cup almonds, chopped
  ¼ cup walnuts, chopped
  2 eggs
  ¾ cup sugar
  3 tablespoons melted butter or margarine
  ½ cup water reserved from soaking apricots or ¾ cup warm water
  ½ cup milk
  1 tablespoon grated lemon rind
  1 tablespoon lemon juice

Grease and flour a 9 × 5-inch loaf pan.

Soak apricots in water to cover 2 hours. If there is water left over, reserve ½ cup. Roughly chop apricots and set aside.

Combine flour, baking powder, salt, and baking soda in a large bowl. Stir in nuts and set aside.

In a separate bowl beat eggs until fluffy, gradually adding

the sugar. Stir in melted butter, apricots, reserved apricot-soaking liquid or ¾ cup warm water, milk, lemon rind, and lemon juice.

Slowly pour the apricot mixture into the dry ingredients, stirring to blend well.

Turn batter into prepared pan and cover with an inverted pan the same size or with a tent of foil. Let stand 15 minutes. Heat oven to 350°F.

Bake covered for 45 minutes. Uncover and continue baking for 15 minutes or until a cake tester comes out clean when inserted in the middle of the loaf.

Turn out of pan and cool completely on a rack. Freeze in airtight wrap. Thaw at room temperature and refrigerate thawed bread.

Hint: Very good spread with cream cheese.

Fruitcake

This is the real made-from-scratch version of fruitcake. When you read through the recipe, you will see why a team effort is so important. Fruitcakes are not difficult to make, but several things must be done; each of them takes time. There are three distinct steps: preparation of the pans, preparation of the fruits and nuts, and preparation of the batter. In addition to the ingredients, you will need plenty of wax paper for lining the bottoms of the pans, vegetable shortening for greasing them, and cheesecloth for wrapping finished cakes.

A few black walnuts would taste wonderful in this cake, if you can find them.

It is important to have all ingredients at room temperature.

   Vegetable shortening
 1 **pound mixed candied fruit, drained if necessary**
 8 **ounces fresh figs cut in ½-inch pieces, stems removed**
 8 **ounces currants**
 8 **ounces raisins**
 2 **cups nuts in large pieces: walnuts, pecans, almonds combined**
 ½ **cup flour for dredging**
 ¾ **cup butter or margarine**

1 **cup sugar**
5 **eggs, well beaten**
1 **cup flour**
½ **cup white cornmeal**
1 **teaspoon salt**
1 **teaspoon baking powder**
1 **teaspoon ground allspice**
½ **teaspoon nutmeg**
½ **teaspoon ground cloves**
½ **cup orange juice**
  Rum, brandy, or bourbon

Grease one 10-inch tube pan or two 7 × 3-inch loaf pans or two 1-pound coffee cans with vegetable shortening. Line bottoms with wax paper (trace shape from pans and cut out with scissors); grease top of wax paper.

Heat oven to 300°F.

Dredge all fruits and nuts in the ½ cup flour and set aside.

Cream butter and sugar together. Add eggs and beat until smooth. Into a separate bowl sift the 1 cup flour and all other dry ingredients together and blend into butter-egg mixture alternately with the orange juice.

Fold dredged fruits and nuts into batter.

Fill prepared pans two-thirds full. Do not overfill. Place in oven and reduce temperature to 275°F. Check after 2 hours, often thereafter. Bake until cake is firm to the touch and starting to draw away from sides of the pan. The cake will be sticky on top.

Let cake cool in pan for 5 minutes; loosen by running a knife around all sides. Turn out on a rack to cool completely bottom side down.

When cake is completely cool, wrap in cheesecloth, folding excess over at the top. Before sealing containers, pour rum, brandy, or bourbon in to soak cheesecloth. Cover with airtight wrap (cakes baked in coffee cans can be put back into clean cans and sealed with the cans' snap-on plastic lids), and store at cool room temperature for at least a month. More time is better. Soak with liquor two or three more times before cake is cut.

Hints: Fruitcakes baked in 1-pound coffee cans weigh about 2½ pounds and are very popular at fund-raising events and for mailing as gifts. Wrap with a strip of gift paper cut to fit between top and bottom ridges of the can, then in heavy brown paper. Address and mail.

Very sharp kitchen shears are the best implement for cutting stems off figs and cutting the figs into pieces.

Don't chop nuts. They make beautiful cross sections when the cake is cut.

Christmas Pudding

This dessert is commonly called plum pudding, a name that gives Americans fits since, as far as they can see, it doesn't contain any plums. Well, it does, only they are dried ones, commonly known as prunes. This recipe doesn't call for even dried plums, but if you like prunes better than raisins or currants, use them in proportion to the amount of currants or raisins you leave out. Use seeded prunes cut into 3 pieces each.

Ask your butcher to grind the suet for you, or do it yourself in a food processor. If necessary, chop the suet very fine by hand.

        2 cups raisins
        2 cups currants
    1½ cups mixed chopped candied citrus peel
        1 large tart apple, chopped
        1 cup flour for dredging
        1 teaspoon ground cinnamon
    ½ teaspoon ground cloves
        1 teaspoon nutmeg
        5 cups fresh bread crumbs
    1½ teaspoons salt
        1 cup brown sugar
    ¼ cup white sugar
    1½ cups very hot water
    12 eggs, well beaten
    1½ cups beef suet, ground
    ¾ cup brandy or cider

Thoroughly grease two 2-quart covered pudding molds, tube pans, or bundt pans.

Dredge fruits in flour; set aside.

Mix spices with bread crumbs, salt, and sugars. Pour hot water over crumbs and let cool completely.

Add eggs and suet and mix well. Add dredged fruits and ½ cup of the brandy and mix thoroughly.

Turn batter into prepared molds or pans and cover tightly. Tie foil securely around pans if you do not have molds with tight lids.

Set up steamer: In a very large pot with a tight lid, place racks to hold puddings. On top of stove bring water to boil in bottom of steamer; keep water below the level of the rack where puddings will rest. Put puddings on racks, tightly cover steamer, and reduce heat so pot steams but does not boil hard. Steam for 6 hours. Add boiling water from time to time to maintain level. Pour it down the side of the pot to prevent splashing.

Puddings are done when they are firm and a cake tester comes out nearly clean (this is a sticky, waxy dough). The tops of the puddings will be sticky. Remove from molds or pans and let cool completely. Pour the remaining ¼ cup brandy or cider over puddings. Store at cool room temperature in airtight wrap until Christmas. Longer storage won't hurt. Add more brandy if puddings look dry during storage.

Hints: To make fresh bread crumbs, remove crusts, if you wish, from day-old white bread. Cut into cubes and pulse in a food processor or blender until fairly fine crumbs form. If you have to do this job by hand, cut bread into cubes as small as possible, then snip with scissors into bowl to make crumbs.

It is traditional to flame Christmas pudding with brandy and serve it with Hard Sauce (page 169).

Fund-Raisers

Local organizations often raise money by selling contributed food at bazaars, church and community events, and school functions. Here are some of the best and easiest candies to donate to fund-raising events and to fill your own candy dishes for the holidays.

Never-Fail Fudge

5 cups sugar
1 teaspoon salt
½ pound butter or margarine
1 can (13 oz.) evaporated milk
24 ounces semisweet chocolate bits
1 can (12 oz.) marshmallow cream
2 teaspoons vanilla extract
1 cup broken pecans or walnuts

Butter two 9 × 13-inch glass baking pans.

In a large heavy saucepan, bring sugar, salt, butter, and evaporated milk to a boil you can't stir down. Adjust heat so that syrup maintains a brisk boil but does not run over the top of the pan. If the syrup subsides and leaves sugary residue on the sides of the pan, carefully wipe it away with a wooden spatula wrapped in a cloth that has been moistened with cold water. Boil for 15 minutes.

Remove syrup from heat. When boiling stops, add chocolate bits and marshmallow cream. Beat until blended and smooth.

Stir in vanilla extract. Fold in nuts.

Pour candy into the prepared pans and let it cool completely. Cut into 1-inch squares. As you take the candy out of the pans, turn each piece upside down so that it can continue cooling and dry a little bit. Then store in airtight wrap at cool room temperature (do not refrigerate). This recipe makes 5 pounds of fudge.

Hint: Be sure to use genuine, not artificial, vanilla extract. It makes world of difference in the finished fudge.

Peanut Butter Fudge

This recipe is so easy it's funny. The fudge, however, is no laughing matter. It has a large following.

4 cups brown sugar
2 cups evaporated milk
1 cup smooth peanut butter
2 teaspoons vanilla extract

Thoroughly butter two 7 × 11-inch glass baking pans.

Bring sugar and milk to a boil in a large heavy saucepan. Let cook to the soft-ball stage (238°F. on a candy thermometer).

Add peanut butter and vanilla extract to syrup and beat until blended and smooth.

Pour candy into prepared dishes. Let cool completely, then cut in 1-inch squares. As you remove the candy from the dish, turn each piece upside down so that the bottom can finish cooling and dry a little.

Store candy in airtight wrap or containers at cool room temperature; do not refrigerate. This recipe makes about 4 pounds of fudge.

Hints: You could add nuts to this recipe, but they seem redundant. You could also add more than a cup of peanut butter.

Many expert candy cooks say they find it difficult to make good candy in stainless-steel or aluminum pans. Too many sugar crystals form on the sides of the pan as syrup cooks. If you have a heavy nonstick or enamel-over-cast-iron pan, by all means use it.

Nut Brittle

1 cup broken nuts, any kind
1 cup sugar
½ cup water
¼ teaspoon cream of tartar
1 tablespoon butter

Place a piece of foil at least 18 inches long on a very flat surface that is heat resistant. Spread nuts evenly over the foil. Leave 2 inches clear all around edges.

Bring all other ingredients to a boil in a large heavy saucepan. Simmer until sugar is melted and the mixture turns honey-colored. Do not overcook. Remove from heat and stir in butter to mix thoroughly.

Pour caramel syrup in a thin stream over nuts. If you have syrup left over, reheat it to melt again, arrange more nuts on a second sheet of foil, and repeat the procedure.

Leave the Nut Brittle undisturbed until it is completely cool and hard. Peel foil away and break brittle into serving-size pieces. Store in airtight wrap at cool room temperature (do not refrigerate). This recipe makes about 1½ pounds of nut brittle.

Hints: Treat the caramel syrup with great respect. It is very, very hot. It will burn badly if it spatters on your skin. Take precautions. If someone is burned, flood the area with cold water until syrup washes away. Open a vitamin E capsule and squeeze the liquid onto the burn, or use the juice from an aloe leaf. If the burn is large, seek medical help.

If you don't have cream of tartar, don't worry. It helps to prevent sugar crystals from forming, but it isn't vital.

You may want to add a pinch of salt to the syrup, even though brittles are often made with salted nuts. It's a matter of taste.

Your life will be easier if you acquire a candy thermometer—or get a new one if yours is very elderly.

Cooking the Neighborhood Jack-o'-Lanterns

Before the Halloween season begins, ask some of your friends and neighbors if they have plans for their jack-o'-lanterns after the holiday. If they don't, ask if you can have them. A very large pumpkin will yield 2 cups puree (the amount called for in most recipes) or more, a small one less than 1 cup.

The day after Halloween, collect the retired jack-o'-lanterns. You will be doing your friends a favor by taking the pumpkins off their hands, yourself a favor by getting free pumpkin puree for the next year, and the environment a favor by recycling an edible.

Examine the jack-o'-lanterns. If any look very tired or grubby, as if the dog has played with them, throw them away. Cut the good ones in 1-inch strips from top to bottom. Clean and scrape off any flesh that has been charred by candles or light bulbs. Remove melted wax and anything else that does not look like the inside of a pumpkin. Sniff. Does it smell wholesome? If so, peel each slice and cut it into chunks 1 to 2 inches long. It is easier to peel the long strips than the whole pumpkin.

Place the pumpkin cubes on a rack in a steamer over water that does not touch the pumpkin (the chunks don't have to be in a single layer). Cover tightly. Steam over boiling water until pumpkin is very tender, about 20 minutes. Test with a cake tester or a small sharp knife. Puree in a food processor or with a potato masher. To help stabilize the puree add 1 teaspoon salt and ½ teaspoon sugar for each pint (2 cups) of pumpkin. Pour the puree into pint-size plastic freezing containers. Cool and seal with airtight lids, squeezing out as much air as possible from containers. Freeze until needed.

Christmas Cookies

During the week after Halloween, while you have the baking equipment out and your hand in, make the Christmas cookies. Bake your traditional family cookies and the ones you trim the tree with. If you don't have any traditional Christmas cookies, ask the best cooks you know. Does anyone you know have a grandmother from another culture? I'll bet she would be delighted to tell you *her* culture's cookie recipes. You could be an adopted Armenian, Croatian, Greek, Hungarian, Serbian, Ukrainian, or whatever for the holidays and start your own tradition. Wrap the cookies tightly and store or freeze as directed in the recipes.

9

❦❦❦❦❦❦❦❦❦❦

Thanksgiving

THANKSGIVING IS THE BEGINNING OF THE SERIOUS HOLIDAY season. Many people say it is their favorite of all.

A Traditional Thanksgiving Dinner

Like all special meals, Thanksgiving dinner requires some planning and organization. The middle of October is not too early to begin thinking about your celebration. Experienced entertainers know that the more they do early, the more they and their guests will enjoy the party.

1. Mid-October:
   Make guest list and get invitations out.
2. By November 1:
   Plan menu.
   Order fresh turkey; reserve frozen bird of the size you need. If your butcher deals with the turkey grower, ask that your turkey be dressed with only the feet removed. There will be a bare, ugly bone below the drumstick, but when the bird is done, it will twist off easily, leaving the drumstick end tender and moist.
3. By November 15:
   Polish your silver if you didn't do so at Halloween. Press linens.
   Order flowers or other table decorations. Order wine.
   Check your candle supply; replenish as necessary if you didn't buy candles at Halloween.
4. One week before Thanksgiving:
   Start stockpiling bread for stuffing; make corn bread (page

34) Let it dry out a day or two. Then store in tightly sealed plastic bags in freezer.

Pick up frozen turkey, if you're using one.

Shop for nonperishable groceries.

Cook ahead any food that you can; store carefully.

Devise your seating plan.

If you are using place cards, make them.

5. Monday before Thanksgiving:

Shop for perishable food.

Continue cooking ahead. For instance, mix dry ingredients for stuffing and refrigerate; make Cranberry Relish.

Pick up fresh turkey if you're using one.

Pick up flowers.

Make turkey broth.

6. Wednesday before Thanksgiving:

Make vegetable puree for Oyster Bisque.

Make batter for rolls.

Clean and trim vegetables.

Make pies and cake if you didn't do it at Halloween.

Lay table after Wednesday dinner.

There! Actually stuffing (always at the last moment before roasting) and roasting the bird and finishing up the fresh vegetables are all you have left to do.

There is no use saying that a big holiday dinner isn't work: it is. But there are tremendous rewards. Forging family traditions, establishing some of your own, seeing people you have missed—all these are things to be thankful for. Now get some rest. Chanukah and Christmas are coming.

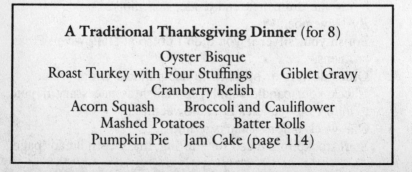

A Traditional Thanksgiving Dinner (for 8)

Oyster Bisque

Roast Turkey with Four Stuffings   Giblet Gravy

Cranberry Relish

Acorn Squash   Broccoli and Cauliflower

Mashed Potatoes   Batter Rolls

Pumpkin Pie   Jam Cake (page 114)

Oyster Bisque

This is a lighter version of a sumptuous dish. Remember it is a first course, so keep serving sizes moderate. It can be made quickly, but you need to serve it as soon as it is finished.

1 tablespoon butter
1 small onion, finely chopped
1 small garlic clove, chopped
1 celery stalk, leaves and all, finely chopped
3 cups milk
2 pints shucked oysters with their liquid
    Salt and pepper

Melt butter in a heavy saucepan. Over low to medium heat, cook onion, garlic, and celery until soft but not browned. Puree the vegetables in a blender or mash them with a wooden spoon.

Return puree to saucepan. Add milk and let the mixture come to a very low simmer. Add oysters and their liquid. Cook only until the edges of the oysters begin to curl.

Remove from heat, taste, and add salt and pepper. Serve at once in warmed bowls.

Roast Turkey with Four Stuffings

For eight people, plan to buy a 12- to 15-pound turkey. Decide whether to use a fresh or frozen bird. If you are using a frozen turkey, start it thawing *well* in advance of the holiday. As Peg Bracken, author of *The I Hate to Cook Book,* said, there is nothing spontaneous about a frozen turkey dinner, and the bigger the bird the less spontaneity you have to work with. Removing the package of giblets as soon as you can get it loose speeds up the thawing process somewhat. If you're using a fresh turkey, check it over carefully and remove any remaining feathers (use tweezers) before roasting.

If you have wonderful broth, you will have great gravy and stuffing. Make the broth well in advance; the fat will rise to the top during refrigeration and will be easy to remove.

You will need 7 or 8 cups of stuffing to fill a bird this size. If there is more than will go inside, bake the rest in a dish during the last half hour of the turkey's roasting time. Money in the bank. Use nonsweet bread in your stuffing. Do not use whole wheat or rye bread; it tends to give the stuffing a sour taste.

Turkey Broth

You can add some chicken giblets to this broth if you want an especially rich stock.

6 cups water
Turkey giblets
1 medium-size onion stuck with 2 whole cloves
1 large carrot, roughly chopped
2 celery stalks, leaves and all, roughly chopped
Bouquet garni: several parsley springs, 3 or 4 peppercorns, 2 or 3 garlic cloves, and 1 bay leaf tied up in a square of cheesecloth
Salt

Heat the water in a large saucepan with a lid. Rinse the giblets with cold water, drain, and drop them into the saucepan. When the water boils, add all other ingredients and reduce heat so that the pot, partially covered, simmers. Remove the liver when it is tender—test it after 10 minutes. Liver can make the gravy rather bitter, so set it aside for another use. Or eat it: cook's reward. Simmer giblets until a knife easily pierces the gizzard, usually about 1 hour.

Let pot cool until you can handle it. Strain the broth (there should be about 4 cups) and discard the vegetables and bouquet garni. Remove giblets from stock and chill. Take the meat off the neck bone before the meat is chilled; it is very difficult to remove meat from very cold bones. Taste broth and add salt.

Refrigerate giblets and broth separately, tightly covered.

Corn Bread Stuffing

     8 cups stale corn bread with toast, rolls, or bagels
         (very good), crumbled
     1 cup chopped onion
     1 cup chopped celery, leaves and all
     2 eggs, lightly beaten
2 or 3 tablespoons butter or margarine, melted
    ¼ cup chopped parsley
     1 teaspoon thyme
     1 tablespoon dried ground sage
     1 cup turkey broth (approx.)
         Salt and pepper

Toss all ingredients together. If you need more liquid, add a little more broth or some water or white wine. You want a crumbly mixture, not a paste. Taste and add salt and pepper.

Stuff turkey. If there is extra stuffing, bake it in a separate pan for 30 minutes at 325°F. in same oven with the turkey.

Hints: If your guests are onion-lovers, by all means use more onions.

When fresh sage is available, use it in place of the dried sage. Taste after adding ¼ cup.

You should not use 8 cups of corn bread alone in this recipe; it will be too crumbly.

Chestnut Stuffing

     7 cups stale white bread and rolls, crumbled
     1 cup chopped celery, leaves and all
    ½ cup chopped fresh parsley
  1½ teaspoons dried rosemary
     1 egg, lightly beaten
     1 cup turkey broth (approx.)
         Salt and pepper
     2 cups shelled cooked chestnuts

Toss bread, celery, herbs, and egg together. Add broth. Taste and add salt and pepper.

Roughly chop and gently fold in chestnuts.

Stuff turkey. Bake extra stuffing in separate pan for 30 minutes at 325°F.

Oyster Stuffing

7 cups stale bread crumbs
1 medium-size onion, chopped
1 celery stalk, leaves and all, chopped
2 tablespoons butter
1 teaspoon thyme
2 teaspoons grated fresh lemon rind
2 tablespoons lemon juice
2 pints oysters with their liquid
  Turkey broth or dry white wine
  Salt and pepper

Put bread crumbs in a large bowl.

Sauté onion and celery in butter until just soft; add to crumbs. Stir in thyme, lemon peel, and lemon juice.

Strain oysters, reserving the liquid. Gently fold oysters into dry ingredients.

Add oyster liquid and stir gently until mixture is crumbly. Use a small amount of turkey broth or wine if you need more liquid. Taste and add salt and pepper.

Stuff turkey. Bake extra stuffing in separate pan for 30 minutes at 325°F.

Sausage Apple Stuffing

1 pound bulk pork sausage or 1 pound link sausage, crumbled
1 cup chopped tart apple
1 small onion, chopped
1 cup chopped celery
2 garlic cloves, finely chopped
6 cups crumbled stale bread, including corn bread
  Turkey broth
  Salt and freshly ground pepper

Crumble sausage into a skillet and cook until it gives up its fat and loses its pink color. Drain thoroughly. Discard fat.

Mix sausage, apple, onion, celery, and garlic into bread. Add enough turkey stock to make a crumbly mixture. Add salt and pepper to taste. Freshly ground pepper is especially important; use lots of it.

Stuff turkey. Bake extra stuffing in separate pan 30 minutes at 325°F.

Roast Turkey

1 turkey (12 to 15 lb.)
Salt and pepper (optional)
Stuffing
Softened butter or soft margarine
Melted butter or margarine for basting

Rinse the turkey well in cold water inside and out and dry it thoroughly. Sprinkle salt and pepper inside and out if you wish.

Fill body and neck cavities of the bird *loosely* with stuffing (it expands). Secure the neck skin to the bird's back with a skewer and tie the legs together. Tuck the wings behind the turkey's back.

Heat oven to 350°F. Put the turkey on a roasting rack in a large baking pan. Rub the breast, wings, and legs with softened butter or margarine. Roast the turkey for 1 hour. Check occasionally. You may want to baste the bird with broth or additional melted butter or margarine.

Reduce heat to 325°F. Allow 30 minutes baking time per pound. A meat thermometer should reach 180°F. when inserted on the inside of the thigh. If you are not using a thermometer, check that the juice runs clear, not pink, when the thigh is pierced with a sharp knife.

When the turkey is done, put it on a platter and keep it warm. The turkey should rest at least 15 or 20 minutes before you carve it.

Hints: A cloth towel will get the outside of the turkey drier than paper towels (wash it before using it for any other purpose). A dry bird roasts to a beautiful even color.

You may want to rub the cavity of the turkey with a cut lemon half. The lemon will counteract the somewhat gamy taste some turkeys (especially frozen ones) develop.

Whether to add salt and pepper is a vexing question. The theory is that salt added before cooking causes the bird to dry out. Use your own judgment and experience.

The larger the turkey, the lower the oven temperature should be. For a 12- to 15-pound turkey, reduce heat to 325°F. after an hour; for a larger bird, even lower. The object is to cook the meat and brown and crisp the skin at the same time.

Your life will be a lot easier if you acquire a meat thermometer.

Place a tent of foil over the turkey while it rests. The foil will keep the turkey warm without making the skin soggy.

Giblet Gravy

Cooked turkey giblets
4 tablespoons fat from roasting pan
4 tablespoons flour
4 cups stock or stock and water
Salt and pepper

Chop the giblets and set aside.

Drain the fat from the roasting pan into a measuring cup. If there is less than 4 tablespoons fat, add butter or margarine to make 4 tablespoons.

Return measured fat to the roasting pan. Put it over medium heat. Stirring constantly with a wooden spoon, add flour. Cook slowly until the mixture is thick and smooth.

Add stock or a combination of stock and water. Bring gravy to a fast simmer, stirring. Be sure to scrape up all the brown bits from the bottom of the pan.

Cook until gravy is thick and smooth. Add the giblets and just heat through. Add salt and pepper to taste.

To serve, stir well and pour into a warmed gravy boat.

Cranberry Relish

1 pound cranberries
2 unpeeled oranges
1 package (4-serving size) raspberry gelatin
1 cup boiling water
¾ cup cold water
3 tablespoons sugar or to taste
½ cup walnuts or pecans broken into small pieces (optional)

Wash and look over cranberries; discard any that look unhealthy. Cut oranges in small pieces, discarding seeds but leaving peel on.

Place fruits in a food processor and chop very roughly. Or put through a food mill.

Dissolve gelatin completely in the boiling water. Add the cold water. Let cool.

Mix chopped fruit and their juices with cooled gelatin. Taste and add sugar cautiously. This relish tastes sweeter cold than at room temperature, and it should be tart.

Stir in walnuts or pecans if you're using them.

Put relish into an attractive glass serving dish with a lid. Refrigerate several hours or overnight. The gelatin thickens the mixture somewhat but does not actually get firm.

Batter Rolls

Hot fresh yeast bread is a fond memory for most of us. If necessary, you can prepare the batter for this yeast bread and store it, covered, in the refrigerator for three or four days.

- 3 **envelopes dry yeast**
- 2 **cups lukewarm water (110°F., or barely warm to the inside of your wrist)**
- ¾ **cup melted butter or margarine**
- 4 **cups self-rising flour (more if needed)**
- 1 **egg, lightly beaten**
- 4 **tablespoons sugar**

In a large mixing bowl dissolve the yeast in the warm water. Let stand 5 minutes.

Add melted butter and flour to yeast and mix well. Stir in beaten egg and sugar. The batter will be about the consistency of heavy cream. If it is thinner, add a little more flour.

Set the batter aside, covered, for several hours or overnight in the refrigerator.

To bake, heat oven to 450°F. Thoroughly grease muffin tins. Stir batter well and fill 12 to 16 cups two-thirds full. Bake for about 25 minutes, until rolls are puffy and golden brown.

Hint: If you need more bread, mix two batches of batter. Doubling the ingredients doesn't work well for this recipe.

Pumpkin Pie

Since pumpkin pie filling is basically a custard flavored with pumpkin puree, the pies are better if made just a day or two before they are to be served. You will need an unbaked 8-inch piecrust (page 115) for each pie. If you have made piecrusts ahead and frozen them, you do not need to thaw them before completing pies. Just place the frozen crusts in pie pans, fill, and check baking time often to make sure filling is done and crusts are nicely browned.

1 can (16 oz.) pumpkin or 2 cups homemade pumpkin
 puree
½ teaspoon ground cinnamon
½ teaspoon ground ginger
¼ teaspoon nutmeg
¾ cup sugar
¼ cup brown sugar
 Dash salt
2 eggs, slightly beaten
1 can (13 oz.) evaporated milk
1 unbaked 8-inch piecrust

Heat oven to 425°F.

Mix all ingredients except crust until smooth and blended and until sugars are dissolved.

Turn filling into piecrust. Do not overfill pan.

Bake at 425°F. for 15 minutes; reduce heat to 350°F. and continue baking 45 to 50 minutes, until piecrust is lightly browned and filling is set. Let cool completely before serving.

Hint: It is normal for filling to puff up during baking, then sink slightly as the pie cools.

Turkey Soup: A Way to Use Everything but the Gobble

When Thanksgiving dinner is over, remove as much meat as possible from the turkey bones. Refrigerate meat and carcass separately, both tightly wrapped. When you have recovered from the holiday, you can enjoy one of the freebies of the season.

Turkey Soup

    Turkey carcass
1 large onion
2 large carrots
2 celery stalks, leaves and all
2 garlic cloves (optional)
3 or 4 parsley sprigs
2 bay leaves
3 or 4 whole peppercorns
1 teaspoon dried thyme
1 teaspoon dried rosemary
    Salt

Break up the turkey carcass into pieces and place the bones in a large heavy soup pot with a lid. Cover by at least an inch with cold water and bring it to a boil.

While water heats, roughly chop vegetables and add to pot. Add seasonings except salt. When water boils, reduce heat so that it barely simmers and cook the soup, covered, until the vegetables are very tender, about an hour. Taste and add salt.

Let the pot cool until you can handle it. Strain broth into a large bowl. Cool and refrigerate, tightly covered. Remove any remaining meat from the bones. Store separately. Discard bones, skin, pieces of fat, vegetables, and spices.

Carefully remove fat from surface of the cool broth. Reheat broth in a large soup pot.

Now be creative—with this soup base you can, add fresh vegetables, pasta, and frozen peas for Turkey Noodle Soup; poach dumplings or matzo balls in it; or thicken the broth slightly and add just enough heavy cream to give it a beautiful color for Cream of Turkey Soup. However you decide to serve the soup, add the meat from the carcass just to heat through. You can also dice some leftover turkey into the soup.

A Small Thanksgiving Party

If you are having only a few guests for Thanksgiving dinner, a turkey, even a small one, is going to provide leftovers for ages. It is possible to prepare a wonderful holiday meal without ending up with a refrigerator full of leftover turkey.

A Small Thanksgiving Feast (for 4)

Consommé with Caviar and Sour Cream
Roasted Cornish Hens with Wild Rice
Giblet Gravy (page 136)
Cranberry Relish (page 136)
Brussels Sprouts with Chestnuts
Watercress Salad   Batter Rolls (page 137)
Pumpkin Chiffon Pie

Consommé with Caviar and Sour Cream

1 **can beef consommé**
1 **very small can lumpfish caviar**
1 **cup sour cream**
4 **small parsley sprigs**
   Lemon wedges

Store consommé in the refrigerator overnight so that it will firmly jell. Spoon jellied consommé into four bouillon cups or small serving bowls.

Add one-quarter of the caviar (about 1 teaspoon) to each bowl.

Spoon about 2 tablespoons sour cream around caviar on top of consommé. Garnish with parsley sprigs and lemon.

Refrigerate until serving time.

Hint: It is a good idea to store all canned stocks in the refrigerator. That way, the consommé will always be jelled; the fat on other stocks will rise to the top of the can so that it can be removed easily.

Roasted Cornish Hens

4 Cornish hens
Softened butter or margarine
Melted butter for basting

Ask the butcher to split the hens in half and remove the backbones. Make broth from bones and giblets, using the recipe for Turkey Broth (page 138).

Heat oven to 350°F.

Rinse and thoroughly dry hens. Arrange on a rack in a roasting pan, skin side up. Rub with softened butter.

Roast hens about 1 hour, basting from time to time with melted butter or broth. Check that juice from a small slit in the thigh is clear, not pink. Let birds rest 10 minutes before serving.

Wild Rice

1½ cups wild rice
1 teaspoon salt
3 cups water

Wash and drain rice; look over and remove any twigs. Set aside.

Put salt and water in a heavy saucepan with a lid and bring to a boil. Gradually stir in wild rice. Return to a boil, cover tightly, and reduce heat as much as possible. Cook about 45 minutes, until rice is tender and all liquid is absorbed.

Remove pan from heat and let stand, covered, for 10 minutes before serving.

Brussels Sprouts with Chestnuts

1½ **pounds fresh Brussels sprouts**
 ½ **pound shelled cooked whole chestnuts**
 2 **tablespoons butter**
   Salt and pepper

Wash and trim Brussels sprouts. Cut a shallow cross in the base of each sprout; the cut will discourage the sprouts from coming apart during cooking.

Steam sprouts over salted water until just tender when pierced with a sharp knife. Do not overcook.

Drain sprouts thoroughly. Remove steamer rack, return to pan and add chestnuts. Just heat through. Stir in butter to coat vegetables. Add salt and pepper to taste.

To serve the main course:

1. Bake rolls.
2. Make gravy using 2 tablespoons each fat, broth, and water.
3. Place wild rice in a mound on a large serving platter. Arrange hens over rice. If there is room, decorate with Brussels sprouts and chestnuts; if not, serve the vegetables in a covered dish. Cover platter with a foil tent and keep warm in a 200°F. oven while guests eat the first course.
4. Put out Cranberry Relish.

If only frozen hens are available, let them thaw completely, then halve them with poultry shears. Remove the backbones. Cutting the hens in half makes them easier to eat and lets them cook faster and more evenly. People with smaller appetites can have half a hen, heartier eaters a whole one.

Pumpkin Chiffon Pie

Even people who don't like pumpkin have been known to enjoy this dessert. It is much easier to make two pies than one. If you can't use both, give one away and make someone truly thankful.

> **2 envelopes unflavored gelatin**
> **½ cup pineapple juice**
> **1 cup pureed cooked pumpkin**
> **1 or 2 tablespoons sugar or to taste**
> **½ teaspoon grated fresh ginger**
> **2 egg whites at room temperature**
> **½ cup powdered skim milk**
> **½ cup very cold water**
> **1 teaspoon lemon juice**
> **¼ cup sugar**
> **2 baked 8-inch piecrusts (page 115), completely cooled**

Soften gelatin in cold pineapple juice for 5 minutes. Then heat until no granules of gelatin show on the back of a spoon. Cool completely. Mix with pumpkin puree. Add sugar to taste. Stir in grated ginger.

Beat egg whites to soft peaks. Set aside.

In a large mixing bowl, combine powdered skim milk, water, and lemon juice. Beat with an electric mixer until very stiff. Blend in the ¼ cup sugar.

Gently fold beaten egg whites and whipped milk into pumpkin mixture. Pile lightly into the cooled piecrusts and refrigerate at once. Allow to stand in refrigerator 2 or 3 hours or overnight for the filling to set.

Hints: Fresh ginger gives this pie a wonderful fresh zing, but if it's not available, use ground dry ginger.

You can make many kinds of chiffon pies on this principle: strawberry, cranberry (you need only the juice), and pineapple. They are low-calorie and low cholesterol.

You could use cookie or graham cracker crusts, but they are a bit too sweet for this delicate filling.

10

🕎🕎🕎🕎🕎🕎🕎🕎🕎

Chanukah

THE FESTIVAL OF LIGHTS CELEBRATES A MIRACLE: A LITTLE BIT of sacred oil lasted until a new supply could be brought, eight days in all.

Chanukah is a special time for children. There are gifts and games; it is a good chance for families and friends to get together. This dinner is scaled for little children; they think the food and decorations in their size are great fun, and they are—and very tasty for all ages. Alas, at about eight or nine years old the bloom goes off this kind of thing for most children. Try to entertain the ones you know will enjoy this sort of meal most—say, from four to seven years old.

Chanukah Dinner for Miniature Gourmets

This is a good menu for birthday parties as well. Just remember to keep an eye out for that year when the honoree has become too sophisticated.

Experienced parents and child care workers know that the younger the children, the fewer of them can be entertained in a party setting. Three three-year-olds with a parent will be enough. Children over five can usually manage quite well. When you plan quantities, keep in mind that the older the children, the larger their appetites are likely to be. Be warned.

You can have fun with the table decorations. Consider featuring a centerpiece of small marzipan animals and gold foil–wrapped candies, Chanukah gelt, a traditional part of children's booty on this holiday. The best part is that for a finale, the children can eat the decorations!

Enjoy! The kids won't be little for very long.

Chanukah Dinner for Miniature Gourmets
(for 6 or 8)

Fried Cornish Hens   Very Small Baked Potatoes
Tiny Peas   Potato Pancakes (Latkes) (page 53)
Little Rolls   Pecan Tassies
Miniature Fruit Marzipan   Chanukah Gelt

Please note that Jewish dietary laws require that meat and milk products *not* be eaten as part of the same meal. To observe the dietary laws, use nondairy substitutes as needed when preparing this menu.

Fried Cornish Hens

Cornish hens (1 hen provides 8 small servings)
Flour
Salt and pepper
Vegetable oil
Chicken stock (optional)

Cut up each hen so that you have 2 wings, 2 drumsticks, 2 thighs, and 2 pieces of breast, cut horizontally to preserve the tiny wishbones. Freeze the giblets and backbones for later use. (Cornish hens make particularly tasty stock).

Mix flour with salt and pepper in a paper bag. Dredge hen pieces in flour mixture.

Heat a large heavy skillet over medium heat. When it is hot, add vegetable oil to a depth of ¼ inch. Add as many pieces of hen, skin side up, as the pan will hold without crowding. Keep heat moderate.

Check pieces in 10 or 15 minutes. When the crust is golden, turn the pieces and continue cooking until the skin side is also brown. The hens should now be tender as well as browned. Transfer the pieces to a heatproof serving platter and let them drain on paper towels while you add more oil and finish cooking the hen parts. Keep finished pieces warm in a 200°F. oven.

If you want the meat to be even more tender, drain oil from skillet thoroughly and add a few tablespoons chicken stock. Partly cover the pan and let the meat steam until it is as tender as you want it to be. Uncover skillet and continue cooking so that the crust can dry out and get crisp again. Then arrange the meat on a platter on towels to drain and keep it warm in a 200°F. oven. Wipe out skillet thoroughly, and continue cooking until all pieces are finished.

Very Small Baked Potatoes

Small potatoes are hard to bake without drying them out. This is the easiest way.

Small Idaho or russet potatoes (not new potatoes), unpeeled
Water to cover

Place potatoes in a large pot with water to cover and bring it to a boil. Reduce heat so that pot simmers until potatoes are almost tender, about 20 minutes.

Drain potatoes, pierce with a small knife or skewer, so they won't explode. Finish cooking in the oven with the rolls for about 25 minutes. They require the same temperature as the rolls: 450°F.

Little Rolls

Make Batter Rolls (page 137). Bake in well-greased 2-inch (or smaller) muffin tins. Watch carefully; do not let burn.

Pecan Tassies

Tassies are like very small pecan pies. Even a little kid can eat a whole one. These individual treats help with the eyes-bigger-than-stomach syndrome that children (and grown-ups) sometimes get. Have all ingredients at room temperature.

½ cup margarine
3 ounces cream cheese or cream cheese substitute
1 cup flour
1 egg
¾ cup brown sugar
1 tablespoon margarine
1 teaspoon vanilla extract
½ teaspoon salt
½ cup chopped pecans

Combine margarine, cream cheese, and flour in food processor with metal blade, or cut margarine and cream cheese into flour by hand, until a ball forms. Wrap in wax paper and chill in refrigerator for at least 30 minutes.

Mix egg, brown sugar, margarine, vanilla extract, and salt. Beat until smooth.

Heat oven to 325°F.

Form chilled dough into 24 balls. Press each with your thumb to make a depression and a fairly thin shell. Put 1 teaspoon chopped pecans into each shell and fill with egg–brown sugar mixture.

Bake the tarts on an ungreased cookie sheet for 25 minutes, until shells are lightly browned. Cool on the cookie sheet on a rack. Very carefully remove tassies to a serving dish. Be careful: they are very fragile.

Hints: Tassies should be made no more than one day before they are to be used. They are not particularly good keepers.

If your guests are very young, set table with smaller-than-usual plates and use salad forks and butter knives. In any case provide plenty of paper napkins so that kids can eat with their fingers.

11

❧❧❧❧❧❧❧❧❧❧

Christmas

CHRISTMAS MAY BE THE MOST TRADITIONAL OF FAMILY holidays in most households. It is a whole *season* to be jolly, so pace yourself accordingly and don't be caught short at the big crunch of Christmas dinner.

If you want to have Christmas party or open house, survey the calendar for Saturday nights and Sunday afternoons. Pick one early in the month. You will probably have more invitations accepted because most other people won't have planned their parties yet. And after your party, you can settle back and accept other invitations.

Planning and preparing ahead are absolutely vital for Christmas. Gird up your loins and get out that clipboard.

1. As soon as possible after Thanksgiving, wash and press holiday linens. You may need to touch them up just before using, but you'll be glad you did the main bulk of the holiday laundry well in advance.
2. First week of December:
   If you have special holiday dishes, find them, unpack them, and get them washed. It's no good to remember them on January 2.
   Check silver; touch up if necessary.
   Plan Christmas party or open house.
   If you haven't done it *yet,* for goodness' sake replenish the candle supply.
   Select and order poinsettias; arrange to have them delivered just before your party or by December 15 latest. The supply gets very picked over if you wait.

Get Christmas ornaments out of storage and check them. It is easier to find ornaments and bulbs earlier than later.

Plan decorations. Line up your source of greenery and a tree.

Order meats. Especially if you are using something unusual, like a goose, you certainly need to order it as early as possible. Standing rib roasts are in heavy demand around Christmas. Get your order in now.

3. Just before your party or by two weeks before Christmas:

Make miniature cream puffs for Croquembouche and party food. Assemble nonedible tree and store carefully.

Finish any baking you didn't get done before.

Order seafood for Paella.

Shop for nonperishable groceries.

Order wine and liquor; have it delivered as soon as possible.

Stores are very busy at this time of year; don't get caught in the traffic jam.

4. One week before Christmas:

Put finishing touches on decorations.

Shop for all but the most perishable groceries.

Go out to a party or a quiet dinner. You deserve a break.

Move special breads made at Halloween from freezer to refrigerator to thaw slowly for Christmas breakfasts.

5. December 22:

Shop for perishable items.

Make Tomato and Leek Harvest Soup.

6. December 24:

Sorry about this, but you need to pick up the standing rib roast and the seafood for the paella. You don't have room to store these really perishable items, and it is safer to leave them at the market until just before using.

Cream Puffs

Cream Puffs are easy. You can use them for Croquembouche, desserts, and party food. They take some concentration for a short time, but the results are way beyond the modest ingredients and will well repay you for your efforts. This recipe makes 96 miniature cream puffs. If you want more, make the recipe again, since the quantites given are much easier to work with than a doubled recipe.

1 cup water
½ cup butter or margarine
¼ teaspoon salt
1 cup flour
4 eggs

Bring water, butter, and salt to a boil in a large saucepan. Stir to make sure butter is completely melted.

Dump flour into the pan all at once. Remove pan from heat and beat hard until a ball forms. If your dough does not form a ball quite soon, put pan back on low heat and continue beating until the ball forms.

Off the heat, add the eggs one at a time, beating after every addition until mixture is smooth. The last egg will take a lot of effort.

Heat oven to 425°F.

Drop measuring teaspoonfuls of dough onto ungreased cookie sheets. Place puffs about 1 inch apart to provide room for expansion.

Bake puffs for 10 minutes; then reduce oven temperature to 350°F. Continue baking until puffs are lightly browned and fairly rigid to the touch, 20 to 30 minutes. Remove from oven and make an opening in each puff with a skewer or small sharp knife so that steam can escape. Return to oven, turn off heat, leave door open a crack, and let puffs dry out for about 10 more minutes.

Transfer puffs to a cooling rack and cool completely. Store in tightly sealed plastic bags or airtight canisters for a few days, or double-bag and freeze.

Hints: Make cream puffs on a dry day. Humidity is their enemy.

A wooden spoon with a comfortable handle is the best implement for beating this recipe. Both in making the paste and integrating the egg you are going to get very familiar with the feel of that handle.

If you have a food processor, turn butter-flour ball into the container fitted with the metal blade. Add eggs, one at a time, through the chute. Pulse after addition until each egg is incorporated. Very swift, but be warned: the processor will be a mess.

Cream puffs filled with sweetened whipped cream are delicious, but if you plan to serve them, have someone help you, because the filled puffs won't keep for more than a few minutes; the cream will release liquid, and the puffs will start to fall apart. Better leave this to an establishment that has a staff.

Profiteroles

One of the nicest and easiest of cream puff desserts is Profiteroles. They are simplicity itself.

Fill cooled cream puffs with vanilla ice cream. Top with fudge sauce or melted chocolate. Store in the freezer until ready to serve. (Assemble them just a short while before serving).

Hint: This is a simple dessert if you have already made the cream puffs, but it's very good. Very impressive. Just remember to clear enough space in your freezer to store the profiteroles.

Basic Pastry Cream

The classic filling for dessert cream puffs is a pastry cream. Here is the basic recipe. This will make enough for one recipe of cream puffs, large or small.

 2 cups milk
½ cup sugar
 4 tablespoons cornstarch
 6 egg yolks
 1 teaspoon vanilla extract

Heat the milk to just below the boiling point. Do not let it boil. (If you have a microwave, this is the time to use it.)

While the milk heats, mix the sugar and cornstarch in the

top of a double boiler. Beat the egg yolks well and mix them into the sugar and starch.

Pour the hot milk in a thin stream over the egg-sugar mixture, stirring rapidly all the while with a whisk.

Put the top of the double boiler over simmering water and cook the mixture, stirring constantly with the whisk, until the cream is thick and smooth. Cool the cream until you can comfortably hold your hand on the bottom of the pan. Add vanilla. Stir and let mixture cool completely.

Fill cream puffs with cool pastry cream using the small plain tip from a cake decorating set, or cut the cream puffs in half horizontally, fill them, and replace the tops.

Hint: The classic topping for filled cream puffs is chocolate. You can't improve on melted semisweet chocolate chips. Let the melted chocolate cool slightly; then pour a tablespoon or two over each large cream puff. Use less for tiny ones.

Chocolate Buttercream

If you are willing to work a little harder, you can make this more complex chocolate pastry cream. It isn't difficult; it just takes some time and a few moments of intense concentration. This cream is also useful as cake filling or frosting; it is used as a filling in several divine tortes. You will need a standard electric mixer.

 6 **egg yolks**
⅔ **cup sugar**
¼ **cup water**
¾ **pound unsalted butter, softened**
 6 **ounces semisweet chocolate, melted and cooled**
 1 **tablespoon framboise, Cointreau, or another liqueur**
   (optional)

In the large bowl of an electric mixer beat the egg yolks until light-colored and creamy, 10 to 15 minutes.

While the egg yolks whip, combine the sugar and water in a small heavy saucepan. Bring the mixture to a boil and cook over moderate heat (do not let it boil over) until a candy thermometer reads 238°F. (soft-ball stage).

With the mixer still running, add the hot sugar syrup to the egg yolks in a thin stream. Continue beating until the mixture is completely cool (the bottom of the bowl may be slightly warm only).

Beat the butter and the melted chocolate into the egg mixture a little at a time. When buttercream is almost firm, add liqueur if you are using it and mix well.

Hint: While you are boiling the sugar syrup, keep the heat moderate. If the syrup boils up near the top of the pan and then subsides, it will leave sugar crystals that may make your buttercream less than smooth.

Croquembouche

Croquembouche is used as a decorative display and is not meant to be eaten. You could, of course, make an extra one to serve after the meal. If so, fill puffs with pastry cream or sweetened whipped cream flavored with a little rum. And plan to devote a large part of the day to assembling it.

Caramel (made from Nut Brittle recipe, p. 125)
Miniature cream puffs

Decide what you want to display your croquembouche on. Given the nature of the caramel, the place you make it is the place it stays. Protect edges of plate or cake stand with strips of wax paper, which you can later remove.

Get a foam cone in a size and shape you like. Cover it with brown paper and build your tree around it. You can plug in some decorations if the foundation shows through.

Make caramel. Keep it hot and liquid over simmering water in the double boiler while you work.

Place a circle of puffs on the display surface to cover the circle you have drawn or to surround the plastic form. A 7-inch circle will use 18 to 20 puffs. Check before you begin gluing them together. When you are ready to start in earnest, dip each puff in caramel on the side you mean to stick to the next one. It is best to start with the bottom row bottom side *down*. More stable. See how the next higher row looks with two fewer puffs. Too skimpy? Try one less puff. Continue building rising circles until the tree looks right. Put it in a safe dry place (do not refrigerate) to cool completely and develop strength.

Decorate the tree in proportion to its size: cinnamon red-hots, tiny silver sugar balls (called dragées), miniature bows of narrow ribbon attached with caramel or straight pins.

When the tree is completely dry and set, slip a large airtight plastic bag over it, and close tightly with a twist tie. Store in a cool dry place until ready to display.

Just before displaying the Croquembouche, decorate platter or cake stand with greenery or paper doilies (cut scallops from the lacy edge to fit the space you have).

The tree will probably nearly clean you out of one batch of puffs. If you are using them as party snacks, make another batch while you have everything out and the food processor messed up anyway. Scrub the cookie sheets with a dry plastic scouring ball and wipe well with paper towels; no need to wash seriously between batches.

Christmas Party or Reception

Make as many of the party foods from the New Year's Eve party as your crowd will need. It is often easier to make a variety of recipes than great big batches of two or three things. That will allow you to offer more variety; all of your guests are sure to find something they especially like. Serve small portions of fruitcake and other sweets for dessert.

You do not need to supply a full open bar at a Christmas get-together. Have eggnog (very festive), both alcoholic and nonalcoholic, mulled wine, and maybe some champagne punch. This will be quite enough. Your guests will probably appreciate your restraint, and you will be glad of the lower cost, as stocking an open bar for a crowd is no light invest-ment. Have a good supply of soft drinks on hand, too, espe-cially if you have underage guests. Make sure there is plenty of coffee.

Specify the hours of your party or reception; that way you can control the crowd (think of the parking!) and the amount of your day or evening that is taken up. When the closing hour approaches, stop refilling cups. When the closing passes, start clearing away. Even the most determined party-stayer will get the message.

Of course your holiday decorations should be in place, but if it is very early in the month, don't worry about not having the tree up. More room for circulating, too.

Gala Christmas Eve Supper (for 8 to 12)

Many families like to do a major portion of their holiday entertaining on Christmas Eve. Often people you want to see can come on Christmas Eve but can't make Christmas Day dinner because of their own family commitments; it is also a festive way to get ready for a late service or midnight mass. Christmas Eve supper is also a good way to start the evening if you plan to open presents then instead of on Christmas morning. Set the hour of your meal to accommodate other activities and enjoy.

Gala Christmas Eve Supper (for 8 to 12)

Tomato and Leek Harvest Soup
Holiday Paella
Tequila Tasters' Relish　　Mixed Green Salad
Fruitcake (page 120)　　Jam Cake (page 114)

Tomato and Leek Harvest Soup

This soup can and should be made ahead. Just reheat gently before serving. Keep servings moderate in size; it is a first course.

　1　**medium-size onion**
　2　**garlic cloves**
　2　**celery, stalks, leaves and all**
　2　**large leeks, thoroughly cleaned**
　3　**or 4 parsley sprigs**

> 2 tablespoons butter
> 4 medium-size potatoes
> 2 large ripe tomatoes
> 4 or 5 cups chicken broth
> 1 bay leaf
> 1½ teaspoons salt (approx.)
>   Parsley sprigs for garnish
>   Yogurt or sour cream (optional)

Peel and chop onion roughly. Peel and halve garlic cloves. Chop celery and leeks roughly. In a heavy soup pot with a lid, cook the onions, leeks, garlic, celery, and parsley in the butter until they are soft but not browned, 10 to 15 minutes over moderate heat. Don't rush.

While the onion mixture cooks, peel and slice potatoes. Core and chop tomatoes. When onions are tender, add potatoes, tomatoes chicken broth, and bay leaf to the soup pot. Cook, covered, at a slow simmer until the vegetables are very tender, 45 minutes to 1 hour. Taste and add salt.

Let cool enough to handle. Remove bay leaf. Strain broth into a large storage container, reserving the vegetables.

Puree vegetables in food processor or blender, adding just enough broth to make the mixture smooth. Do this in several batches if necessary. Carefully and thoroughly mix vegetable puree into broth. Refrigerate, tightly covered, until just before serving time.

Gently heat soup almost to a boil. Garnish each bowl with a sprig of parsley and, if you wish a dollop of yogurt or sour cream.

Hint: This soup is also good served cold. Try it some hot September evening. It is very good with croutons.

Holiday Paella

If your group observes a Christmas Eve fast, make the paella entirely with fish and shellfish.

You will need a really large shallow pan for paella. A very large wok will do, something like that. Remember, the paella is going to be served from the pan it was cooked in.

4 slices bacon cut in 1-inch pieces or 4 ounces salt pork cut in ½-inch cubes
1 large onion, sliced thin
4 or 5 garlic cloves, minced
6 chicken breasts or 6 thighs
Flour
Salt and pepper
Chorizos (optional)
3 cups white rice
½ cup dry sherry (optional)
½ bunch parsley
2 or 3 strings saffron
4 cups chicken broth, clam juice, or mixture of both
6 lobster tails, slit up the middle of the bottom and cut in 3 or 4 pieces
12 large raw shrimp in shells
12 raw hard-shell clams
2 dozen sea scallops cut in half
12 mussels (optional)
1 package (10 oz.) frozen tiny peas, thawed
1 can (10 oz.) artichoke hearts packed in water
Red bell pepper or canned pimiento strips

In the paella pan, gently cook bacon or salt pork until browned. Remove from pan and drain well.

In the bacon fat cook onion and garlic until soft but only barely browned. If more fat is needed, use olive oil.

Dredge chicken in flour seasoned with salt and pepper. Remove onion and garlic from pan with a slotted spoon and set aside. Brown the chicken, keeping heat moderate, on both sides. Return bacon, onion, and garlic to pan with chicken. Cover and cook over very low heat for 10 minutes. Remove chicken, bacon, onion, and garlic; set aside. If you are using chorizos, cut them in ⅛-inch slices. Sauté separately in a dry skillet over low heat until fat (lots of it) is given up and sausage slices are browned. Set aside to drain. Discard fat.

Rinse rice for several minutes in cool water. In a large heavy saucepan bring 6 cups water to a boil. Parboil for 15 minutes, keeping just at a simmer.

While rice cooks, drain and discard fat from the paella pan and deglaze pan with 3 or 4 tablespoons of the dry sherry, or use water. Chop parsley and add to pan with saffron. Cook in the deglazing liquid until parsley is wilted and the saffron gives up its color, 5 to 10 minutes. Keep heat moderate.

Drain rice and add to paella pan. Add about 2 cups of the broth to pan. The rice should be barely covered with liquid. Bring to a boil. Cover (use foil if your paella pan does not have a lid) and reduce heat so mixture simmers. Cook about 15 minutes, until rice is almost tender.

About 45 minutes before serving, heat oven to 350°F. Return chicken and onion-garlic mixture to paella pan. Bury chicken in rice. Arrange all cleaned, rinsed, and dried shellfish and chorizos decoratively on top. Add thawed peas. Cut artichoke hearts in quarters and add to pan. Add remaining broth. Cover and bake at 350°F. for about 30 minutes. All the shellfish is done when the shells of the lobster tails turn bright red and the scallops are opaque. Do not overcook; the shellfish will just get tough.

Decorate the finished paella with red pepper or canned pimiento strips. Sprinkle with remaining dry sherry, if you wish.

Hints: If you are making all-chicken paella, of course you would use all chicken broth, no clam broth.

While this recipe may seem rather daunting at first glance, it is really just a series of simple steps. You can start early in the day so that only the final assembly needs to be done before the meal.

French or Italian loaves are good with paella. Just heat and serve.

Tequila Tasters' Relish

If you go to a tequila distillery in Mexico, you will probably be offered a relish to cleanse your palate between tasting samples. This condiment is very refreshing, especially with paella.

6 cucumbers
6 oranges
1 tablespoon chili powder

Use cucumbers that do not have to be peeled if you can. Cut the cucumber in ⅛-inch slices.

Peel and section the oranges. It is important to remove the white membranes as completely as possible. It does not matter if you tear up some of the sections.

Mix cucumber slices and orange sections. Sprinkle with chili powder to taste. It will probably take about 1 tablespoon for relish for 8 to 12, but mix and taste.

Cover tightly and refrigerate until serving time. Relish can be made a few hours ahead but should not stand overnight.

Hints: Provide small plates for relish. It would not be nice to have to juggle it on the plate with the hot paella.

Tequila and beer are the traditional drinks with this meal—tequila before, beer during. Give each tequila drinker half a lime and a salt shaker. Here's the ritual: sprinkle some salt on the back of your hand between the thumb and forefinger. Bite into the lime to get some juice, then lick some salt, then drink a sip of tequila. Somehow the combination is better than the parts. The tequila goes down tasting almost like melted butter.

I hope you have your cleanup crew lined up. The chief cook should not have any serious work to do until preparations for Christmas dinner begin the next morning.

Christmas Morning Breakfast

If you can arrange it, have a deputy start the coffee and take the breads out of the refrigerator. Put a pitcher of juice on the table along with sugar, milk, and butter, and let people serve themselves as they drift in.

If you feel you should prepare something hot for breakfast, fight the urge very hard. If you still must, these recipes are useful, impressive, and easy. These recipes will serve 6 or more people.

Christmas Morning Breakfast

Popovers   Cinnamon Rolls
Cranberry Bread (page 118)
Pumpkin Bread (page 118)
Apricot Nut Bread (page 119)
Breakfast Casserole
Coffee   Juice

Popovers

Popovers are easy; a mystique has grown up around them that is not at all deserved. They are good; they are impressive. They are not tricky.

Vegetable shortening
1 cup flour
½ teaspoon salt (approx.)
2 large or 3 medium eggs
½ cup milk
½ cup water
1 tablespoon vegetable oil

Heat oven to 425° F. Put about 1 teaspoon solid vegetable shortening into each of eighteen 3-inch muffin cups and place in oven to heat.

Put all remaining ingredients into the container of a blender. Process just enough to make a smooth batter.

Fill heated muffin cups about half full of batter. Return to oven and bake for about 25 minutes. Popovers should be puffed and nicely browned. You may want to pierce each one with the blade of a small sharp knife so as to let them dry out a little. Turn off heat, leave oven door open a crack, and let popovers sit in the oven a few more minutes.

Hints: Mixing the batter in the blender makes it smooth and relaxes the gluten in the flour.

You will recognize this as the basic recipe for pancakes, too. Pancakes also benefit very much from being mixed in the blender. The first pancake is as delicate and elastic as the last one is.

Using half milk and half water will make a more tender product. Some experts use water only. See which version you like best.

This is also the recipe for Yorkshire Pudding. You just bake all of the batter in one big pan greased with the roast drippings.

Almost Instant Cinnamon Rolls

 1 **package (8 to 12) dairy-case croissant dough**
 ½ **cup brown sugar**
 2 **teaspoons cinnamon**
   Pecan pieces (optional)

Heat oven to 425°F. or to temperature specified on croissants package. Thoroughly butter an 8 × 8-inch baking pan or dish. Add brown sugar and set in oven to melt.

Open the package of croissant dough, but do *not* unroll it. Cut the roll crosswise into 12 slices.

When brown sugar is melted, take the pan out of the oven and sprinkle with cinnamon. Add the nuts, if you wish. Arrange slices of dough on top. Return to oven and bake until rolls are puffed and lightly browned, 15 to 20 minutes.

Turn rolls out onto a serving dish at once. If you let them stand in the pan, they will *never* come out!

Hint: The rolls will come out looking prettier if they touch in the baking pan.

Breakfast Casserole

If you feel you must put something on the table for the sausage-and-eggs-and-homefries group, this casserole is good and hearty. It can and should be put together the night before.

4 or 5 **slices white bread**
      1 **pound bulk sausage, browned and drained**
      1 **cup grated cheddar or Swiss cheese**
6 to 8 **eggs**
      1 **cup milk**
      1 **teaspoon dry mustard**
        Freshly ground black pepper
      2 **cups diced potatoes (optional)**

Cut each slice of bread into quarters and remove the crusts if you want to. Arrange the bread in a buttered 9 × 13-inch casserole dish. Place sausage on bread and spread cheese on top of sausage.

Beat eggs with milk, dry mustard, and a generous amount of pepper. Pour over casserole.

Add diced potatoes if you are using them.

Cover tightly and refrigerate several hours or overnight.

Bake at 400°F. for 35 to 40 minutes. Cheese will rise to top. It should be be bubbly and lightly browned. Serve at once.

Hints: A 9 × 13-inch casserole can be cut into 6 or 8 servings. If you have a big crowd, make two casseroles.

This dish is also a good one for supper. In that case, use 2 cups mixed diced carrots, onions, bell peppers, and potatoes instead of all potatoes.

A tablespoon or two of diced or minced onions would probably be very good in the breakfast version, too.

Now you have been virtuous to a fault. Go back to bed until time to put the roast on.

You may want to set up the coffee maker so that it only has to be turned on in the morning or after dinner or whenever. Your coffee will probably taste better if you use bottled spring water rather than tap water. Unless you have exceptionally good-tasting tap water, bottled water is definitely a worth while investment when you set up coffee and tea ahead of time.

Christmas Dinner

You're almost there. This is the last big push of the year— unless you take a very severe view of New Year's Eve as the last push. In any case, you have done much of the work for this meal ahead of time.

Many families feel that having turkey once a year on Thanksgiving is quite enough, but if your family loves turkey, serve it again. Why not? If you would like something different and very festive, try this menu.

Christmas Dinner (for 12)

Individual Crab Soufflés   Cold Cucumber Soup
Standing Rib Roast of Beef
Yorkshire Pudding   Beef Gravy
Broccoli   Baked Onions in Cream
Holiday Salad with French Dressing
Selection of Holiday Desserts
Hard Sauce

Individual Crab Soufflés

This recipe serves 6, so you will need to make it twice for 12. It's much easier to work with these quantities than to double the recipe.

1 pound crabmeat
2 tablespoons each flour and butter
1 cup milk
½ cup mayonnaise
3 egg yolks
   Salt and pepper
2 teaspoons grated lemon peel
1 teaspoon lemon juice
   Grated Parmesan cheese
   Paprika
3 egg whites

Heat oven to 425°F.

Carefully look over crabmeat. Make sure to remove all the bits of shell and cartilage.

Melt butter over moderate heat in a heavy saucepan. Add flour and stir to form a smooth paste. Cook for 5 minutes, stirring constantly. Add milk and continue cooking until sauce thickens, about 5 more minutes. Sauce will be only moderately thick. Add mayonnaise and egg yolks when sauce is thick and has cooled slightly. Season with salt and pepper to taste, lemon peel, and lemon juice. Add crabmeat. Taste the mixture and adjust seasonings if necessary.

Beat egg whites until stiff and glossy. Do not overbeat. Carefully fold egg whites into crab mixture.

Thoroughly butter 6 individual soufflé dishes or custard cups and sprinkle them with grated Parmesan cheese. Divide batter among them and sprinkle with paprika. Bake about 25 minutes or until soufflés are puffed and lightly browned. Serve at once.

Hints: The soufflés need the same oven temperature as the Yorkshire Pudding. Put souffles in about 10 minutes ahead of pudding so that there will be time to eat them before the pudding is ready.

If you are daring you might want to use cayenne instead of paprika, but use a light hand. Place the small soufflé dishes or custard cups on a cookie sheet before you bake them. They'll be much easier to retrieve from oven.

Provide small seafood cocktail forks or demitasse spoons to eat these tiny treasures with.

If you ever want to make a large soufflé—say, for a supper party—from this recipe, bake it in a 1-quart soufflé dish, similarly buttered and sprinkled with cheese. It will serve 6 as a first course, 4 as a main course.

Cold Cucumber Soup

There is no getting around the fact that Crab Soufflés are rich and filling. If you want something lighter, or if you live in a warm climate, you might consider serving this cold soup as a first course instead of the soufflés. This one is pretty and tasty, and it won't break your calorie bank. Cold soups are the hostess's friend, since they can be put on the table before the guests are summoned, eliminating one pass-me-your-bowl bottleneck.

Make two batches to serve 12.

> 2 **chicken bouillon cubes**
> 1 **quart plain yogurt**
> 2 **scallions, including the green part, roughly chopped**
> 3 **cucumbers**
> 2 **garlic cloves, peeled and roughly chopped**
> ½ **bunch fresh dill (optional)**
> 3 or 4 **parsley sprigs**
> **Cucumber slices for garnish**

Combine all ingredients in the container of a blender. Process until smooth. Serve cold garnished with a cucumber slice.

Standing Rib Roast of Beef

The comforting thing about a big impressive hunk of good meat is that it *is* impressive. It's also usually a lot easier to cook than smaller cuts, and it's sure to please your guests. The scary thing is that it is usually expensive and you get that feeling that nothing had better go wrong. Relax. Nothing will. This is the easy part of the meal.

When you order your roast, ask the butcher to separate the meat from the rib and backbones and tie the roast for cooking. That way, you can carve the meat as simply as you would cut a cake, but the meat gets the benefits of cooking next to the bones. If you want to serve a rib on the plates, have the butcher cut the backbone between each rib so that you can carve that way. In either case, the meaty side of the roast should have a nice layer of fat, whether attached to the meat or carefully tied over it. The fat will baste the roast as it cooks and make the flavoring for the Yorkshire Pudding.

1 standing rib of beef roast (8 to 10 lbs., about 6 ribs)
Salt and pepper (optional)
1 garlic clove peeled and cut in half (optional)

Take roast out of refrigerator; wipe with damp paper towels to clean surface and remove any bone dust. Let stand on counter, unwrapped, for an hour or two to warm up a bit.

Heat oven to 400°F.

Season the roast with salt and pepper if you wish. Rub all over with cut garlic clove if your crowd likes it.

Put roast in an open roasting pan, standing it on its own bones; they make the perfect rack for roasting.

Put roast in oven and immediately reduce heat to 350°F. Bake for 1 hour. Then reduce heat to 300°F. Allow 20 minutes per pound in all for rare meat, 30 minutes per pound for well done. If you have a meat thermometer, insert in thickest portion of meat toward end of roasting time. Take roast out when thermometer reads about 110°F. for really rare beef, 150°F. for well done meat. The meat will continue to cook for some time after it leaves the oven, so do not overcook. Even a very rare roast will have end slices that are fairly well done. You can cook one or two of the ribs longer if you have serious fans of well-done beef.

When the roast is done, remove it from the oven and cover loosely with a tent of foil. Let it rest for at least 20 minutes to reabsorb juices and finish cooking. Fortunately that is just the amount of time you need to finish the Yorkshire Pudding.

Yorkshire Pudding

This is our old friend popover dough, a.k.a. pancake batter (page 161).

Heat over to 425°F.

Pour enough fat from the roast pan into two 9 × 13-inch shallow casseroles to cover bottoms generously. Put the pans into the oven to get very hot while you mix two batches of popover dough. Pour one batch into each pan. Bake a few minutes apart so that the second pan will be ready when the first one has been served.

Beef Gravy

When the Yorkshire Pudding is well under way, put the roast on the serving platter. Let stand covered with foil tent, while you make gravy. If you run out of beef fat from the roast, use butter or margarine, not oil, to make gravy. *For each cup of gravy:*

1 tablespoon flour
1 tablespoon fat
1 cup beef stock or broth
   Salt and pepper (optional)

Put roasting pan over direct heat, keeping temperature moderate. Add flour and fat, stirring and scraping all the time to get brown bits up from bottom of pan.

When roux is nicely browned and thickened slightly, add the stock. Stir until gravy thickens. Taste and add salt and pepper if you wish.

Pour gravy into a warmed gravy boat or bowl and keep warm. Cover with plastic to prevent a skin from forming on gravy. Stir well before serving.

Hints: If you have a microwave, you can use it to continue to cook the roast for the well-done contingent. It will also perfectly reheat and refresh second servings of Yorkshire Pudding or leftover pudding—but don't count on having any!

As soon as the meal is over, collect all bones, wrap them, and refrigerate them. They are going to reappear as Boxing Day Deviled Beef Bones. Don't worry about hygiene; they are going to get *very* hot before you see them again.

Baked Onions in Cream

This recipe is so good that it is hard to recommend it highly enough. From simple ingredients comes a feast. For 12 you'd better make 2 recipes. However much you make, there is never any left over.

4 cups thinly sliced yellow onions
4 tablespoons butter or margarine
2 eggs
1 cup heavy cream
Salt and pepper
¾ cup grated Parmesan cheese

In a heatproof, ovenproof 1-quart casserole, sauté onions in butter until they are wilted and barely browned.

Beat eggs and cream together just to mix thoroughly. Pour over onions. sprinkle with salt and pepper to taste. Just before baking, sprinkle with Parmesan cheese.

Bake in a 425°F. oven for 30 minutes. The casserole should be nicely puffed and lightly browned.

Hint: You can make this casserole ahead of time except for sprinkling on the cheese and baking it (at the same temperature the Yorkshire Pudding requires). Just cover the dish tightly and refrigerate.

Holiday Salad with French Dressing

The main function of this salad is to clean the palate and provide something crunchy. The French dressing is the real thing. You don't often have the occasion to make enough salad dressing to do it right. Now you do. For this salad, choose the nicest your produce market offers. Use a mixture of Boston lettuce, spinach, celery leaves, endive—whatever looks crisp and beautiful.

8 cups mixed greens
1 cup extra virgin olive oil
1¼ cup white wine vinegar with tarragon
1 tablespoon Dijon-style mustard or 1½ teaspoons dry
**   mustard**
1 teaspoon salt

Trim, wash, and dry the greens thoroughly. Wrap greens in a towel, put in a plastic bag, and store in the refrigerator. You can do this up to 24 hours ahead of time.

Place the remaining ingredients in the container of a blender and process until the mixture is creamy. Refrigerate the dressing covered, until serving time.

To finish salad, tear greens into bite size pieces and place in large bowl. Pour no more than half the cold dressing onto the greens and toss to coat each leaf thoroughly. If you need more dressing, add it sparingly. You don't want to drown the greens. Pass the pepper mill with the salad.

Store any extra dressing, tightly covered, in refrigerator. To serve later, shake to remix or spin again in the blender.

For dessert, you truly have an embarrassment of riches. Surely now is the time to bring forth the Christmas Pudding (page 122) which has been stored away since Halloween, getting better every day. Pound cake? Why not? Fruitcake, you bet. Some Christmas cookies with eggnog ice cream? Very good. (Buy the ice cream.)

Hard Sauce is the traditional accompaniment to Christmas Pudding. To be at its best, it needs to be made the day it is to be used. It isn't difficult and doesn't take very long.

Hard Sauce

1 cup butter at room temperature
1 cup sifted confectioners' sugar
3 or 4 tablespoons brandy or rum

Cream butter and sugar together. Add brandy stirring until mixture is very smooth but not liquid. Beat until light and fluffy.

Refrigerate until mealtime. When ready to serve, beat again to restore light texture and softness.

Hint: Although rum is a traditional flavoring in cakes, puddings, and hard sauce, many people find it has a medicinal aftertaste. Brandy is very good. Bourbon is also good. Dry sherry? A matter of taste.

If that is not a dinner that will knock twelve people's socks off, I don't know what would. Aren't you glad you did that baking at Halloween? Don't you feel great that you and your guests have a Christmas to remember with the best? Well done. Relax. Tomorrow is pretty well taken care of.

The Alternative Bird

It's always something, as Gilda Radner used to say. If roast beef does not appeal to you and you long for a bird—so long as it isn't a turkey—you have some other choices available. Especially if your group is six or smaller, these alternatives may be just what you need.

Duck Marinated with Fruit and Red Wine

A duck (or duckling, as is usually for sale in supermarkets) actually serves only two or three people. So if you have six people to dinner, two or three ducks will probably do. If you use frozen birds, leave plenty of time for them to thaw completely before marinating.

1 duck or duckling (4 to 6 lbs.)
2 cups *good* dry red wine
1 tart apple, cored but not peeled, roughly chopped
1½ cup dried apricots cut in thin slices
2 tablespoons orange or tangerine rind cut in slivers
6 seeded raw prunes cut in quarters
1 teaspoon salt
1¼ cup brown sugar

1 **small onion, roughly sliced**
2 **whole cloves**
6 **dried hot peppers or black peppercorns, crushed**
Soy sauce (optional)

Wipe duck with a damp paper towel. Make sure oil sack at the top of the base of the tail has been removed. (You will see a tiny incision.)

Mix all ingredients except duck thoroughly. In some recipes, it doesn't make much difference what kind of wine you use. In this one it does, because the duck is in contact with the wine all the time it marinates. Spring for the good stuff.

Cut wing tips off duck and freeze with giblets for later use. Place duck in a heavy plastic bag. Add marinade. Seal bag tight with a twist tie. Put bag containing duck and marinade into another plastic bag and seal it also. Place the double-bagged duck on a plate or in a bowl and marinate in refrigerator for up to 2 weeks. Turn bags when you think about it.

When you're ready to roast the duck fish it out of marinade; reserve marinade for gravy later. Dry duck thoroughly inside and out. Clip skin on breast and legs with manicure scissors in a pretty pattern; make lots of snips.

Heat oven to 325°F.

Place duck on a rack in a deep (at least 3 inches) roasting pan. Roast until duck is nicely browned, about 30 minutes per pound. There will be a very great deal of fat; treat it with respect because it is very hot. Let it cool naturally. It will congeal into pure white fat. Save it. It is excellent for any cooking: cookies, piecrust, basting other birds. Store it in covered containers in the coldest part of the refrigerator.

Let duck rest for 15 minutes. Meanwhile, remove solids from marinade and put them in the container of a food processor or blender. Add just enough liquid marinade to make a smooth gravy. Heat to just below boiling and pass in a sauce boat. Add some soy sauce if salt is needed.

Hints: Directions for roasting duck and goose often say to pierce the skin at frequent intervals with a skewer. The trouble with that is that those little holes heal as the bird cooks. Little snips with manicure scissors do not heal. They show up as tiny chevrons on the skin of the finished bird and look quite acceptable. They drain a lot more fat than punctures.

The easiest way to cut up a roast duck is with poultry shears. Ducks are not really susceptible to carving conventionally since they have a fairly thin layer of meat over a big body cavity. The large cavity is one of the reasons they can float. So show your whole bird, then cut it into serving pieces with shears.

A pretty decoration for the serving platter would be raw dark greens such as kale or spinach and some small fruits— maybe a few bunches of grapes. Use your imagination.

If the fat in the pan begins to burn or if the duck is browning too fast for the amount of time you think it will need, reduce the oven heat to 300°F. The last thing you want is to overheat this bird.

Marinated duck is vaguely Oriental in origin. This vegetable dish tastes especially good with it and is simplicity itself to make.

Snow Peas and Water Chestnuts

2 packages (10 oz. each) frozen snow peas or 1½ pounds fresh snow peas
1 can (6 oz.) water chestnuts
  Soy sauce
  Peanut oil
  Salt and pepper

If you are using frozen snow peas, take packages out of the freezer and let them thaw for an hour or two. If you have fresh snow peas, wash and string them, drain thoroughly, and set aside.

Drain the water chestnuts and cut them in half.

Heat a saucepan over medium heat. Add a tablespoon or two of water. Put in snow peas and simmer them, covered, 3 or 4 minutes.

Add water chestnuts and just heat through.

To serve, pass soy sauce, peanut oil, and salt and pepper.

An especially good vegetable dish with any festive winter meal is Turnip and Apple Casserole. Even people who say they hate turnips will lap this one up.

Turnip and Apple Casserole

>   2 large or 3 medium turnips
>   2 large tart apples, such as Granny Smith or Rome
>   Beauty, peeled
>   2 tablespoons butter
>   Dash salt
> 2 or 3 tablespoons brown sugar
>   1 medium-size onion sliced very thin
>   Buttered bread crumbs (optional)

Peel turnips and slice them a little less than ¼ inch thick. Cut each slice in half or quarters. Slice apples slightly thicker.

Steam turnips on a rack above boiling salted water for 10 minutes.

Heat oven to 350°F.

Butter an 8-inch casserole with a lid with 1 tablespoon butter. Spread half of the turnips in the casserole and top them with half of the apples. Sprinkle lightly with salt and brown sugar. Add sliced onion. Repeat layering procedure with remaining ingredients.

Cover and bake 20 to 30 minutes, until a fork goes easily through the turnips. Uncover. Top with buttered bread crumbs, if you wish, and dot with remaining tablespoon of butter. Run under broiler just before serving to toast crumbs.

Roast Goose

Another alternative bird is goose. Very traditional, very good. A goose, like a duck, will serve only a few people because there is so much cavity and so little meat on each bird. A 6- to 8-pound goose will serve 6 average eaters or 8 people with very light appetites. Prepare for roasting as you would an unstuffed turkey. Roast at 325°F. for about 30 minutes a pound.

As with ducks, the secret is to keep the heat low; you don't want to overheat the fat as it cooks out or brown the skin faster than the meat is cooking. Tie the legs together so that the goose will look presentable, and put the bird on a rack in a deep roasting pan. Some recipes recommend stuffing the goose. This is a bad idea. So much fat is going to be rendered that the stuffing will be a soggy mess. Cut an onion in half, stick a couple of whole cloves into it, and place it in the cavity of the goose. Make whatever stuffing you fancy and bake it in a cake pan alongside the goose for the last 45 minutes.

Snip the skin as suggested for duck. Save the beautiful white fat for other cooking projects.

Goose cries out for simple boiled potatoes to offset its richness. The traditional vegetable dish to serve with it is Red Cabbage and Apples.

Red Cabbage and Apples

1 medium-sized head red cabbage
3 tart green cooking apples such as Granny Smith
1 tablespoon butter
Salt and pepper

Wash cabbage and remove wilted leaves. Cut into 6 or 8 wedges. If you want to, remove part of the core from each wedge. Arrange cabbage wedges in a heavy pot with a lid.

Core but do not peel the apples. Cut into wedges vertically and put between cabbage wedges in heavy pot. Add butter and salt and pepper and pepper to taste.

Bring pot to spluttering on high heat. Immediately cover and reduce heat so pot barely simmers. Cook about 15 minutes, until the cabbage can be easily pierced with a sharp knife but is still tender-crisp. If the cabbage is not cooking at the rate you expect, add a tablespoon of water, cover, and continue cooking a few minutes. Do not overcook. Serve very hot.

Hints: Baked Onions in Cream will taste good with duck or goose, as will Holiday Salad.

If you feel you need bread in addition to the meat and vegetables, try Batter Rolls (page 137) or heat a loaf or two of French or Italian bread from the bakery.

Goose gravy is a seductive thought but don't try it. The fat doesn't taste that great in gravy. Serve a tart condiment such as Cranberry Relish (page 136) or red currant jelly on the side.

Hint: Keep the dessert fairly light after this heavy meal. Lemon ice would be good, maybe with some cookies.

If you are having very, very special people to dinner—think of a grandmother you dearly love—you might want to make Apricot Ice Cream. Be prepared for the honored one to move in with you after tasting this heavenly dessert.

Apricot Ice Cream

2 **cans apricots (16 oz. or 17 oz. each), drained and pitted**
2 **cups heavy cream**
¾ **cup sugar**
2 **tablespoons lemon juice**
2 **tablespoons Grand Marnier**
1 **tablespoon frozen orange juice concentrate**
Mint sprigs or unblanched almonds (optional)

Puree the apricots and set aside.

Bring cream to a boil. Add sugar and stir until completely dissolved.

Add apricot puree to cream mixture. Cool and add remaining ingredients.

Cover and chill thoroughly. Then freeze, tightly covered, at least overnight. A few hours before serving, turn into the container of a blender or food processor and process until smooth. Refreeze.

Serve small portions—this ice cream is very rich. It is pretty garnished with a sprig of mint or an unblanched almond.

Hints: This recipes makes 1 quart of ice cream. If you want to serve it to a larger group or have some on hand, make the recipe twice. It will keep well in the freezer for up to a month.

Use Cointreau in this recipe if you must—but Grand Marnier is better.

If you want to go for overkill, you could serve Apricot Ice Cream in cookie bowls. Make simple sugar cookie dough, cut it in circles, and bake draped over inverted custard cups. *Definitely* be prepared for guests so honored to take up permanent residence.

You can used dried rather than canned apricots in this ice cream if you wish. The flavor is, if anything, more intense. Soak 1 pound dried apricots for several hours or overnight in water to cover. Drain when ready to use. Puree as you would canned apricots.

Consider buying an ice cream freezer that can be stored in the freezer until needed. Put the ingredients into its container, turn the handle, and in a very short time you'll have perfectly mixed and frozen ice cream. These devices are inexpensive and they really work. They are also good for simple ices made of fruit and sugar or fruit juice. You can make these ices when the fruit is lush and you need something cold and refreshing.

Boxing Day Deviled Beef Bones

Remember those bones you squirreled away after Christmas dinner? They are going to perform again. If they were picked very clean, or if there aren't enough for your crowd, your butcher probably has lots of them. Most butchers remove bones from meat for all those people who don't want the bones. This fact is also good to remember when you want to make brown stock. Ask on Friday or early Saturday.

Beef ribs and backbones
2 tablespoons dry mustard
1 large onion, minced
1 teaspoon salt
2 teaspoons beef broth or water
Freshly ground pepper

Heat oven to 400°F.

Lay beef bones in a shallow baking pan large enough to hold them without overlapping.

Mix mustard, onion, salt, and liquid to make a thick paste.

Rub each and every bone with mustard mixture. Grind pepper over bones freely.

Start cooking raw bones 15 minutes ahead of cooked bones. Bake raw bones for 45 minutes. Add roast bones and cook for another or 30 minutes until coating is brown and bones are thoroughly hot. Serve at once with barbecue sauce, baked potatoes, and a salad. Hold bones in your hand to gnaw. Provide plenty of napkins. Beer is the drink with Deviled Bones.

Whether you celebrate Boxing Day by presenting gifts to the people who work for you (they like money) or just use the day to unwind, you can eat up the lovely leftovers from the holiday dinner.

Hints: Leftover turkey, duck, and goose are equally good deviled. Since they are thoroughly cooked already, they will need only 25 to 30 minutes in the oven. Same menu, same beer.

Please remember that bones are *not* good for household pets. They splinter, and you could have a tense emergency run to the vet if you let your pets chew on the bones. Remember also that cats love the string used to truss fowl or roasts, but it is bad, bad, *bad* for them. Put it in an inaccessible garbage container as soon as you remove it from meat.

If there is a long gap between garbage pickups around the holidays, you could do worse than to double-bag the smelliest garbage and freeze it (unless it is cold enough outside to freeze it) until time for pickup. Your freezer should be fairly empty after the extravaganza. Use it to good purpose.

Now you can rest until New Year's Eve. Next year, work hard to get invited to someone else's bash. Until then, happiest of holidays and Happy New Year. May yours be the best ever.